Heanor
Schooldays

A Social History

by

Narvel S. Annable

Belper 1998

British Library Cataloguing in Publication Data.
A catalogue record for this book is available
from the British Library

ISBN 0 9530419 1 3

Published by
Narvel S. Annable
44 Dovedale Crescent
Belper
Derbyshire DE56 1HJ.

Printed by:

MOORLEY'S Print & Publishing
23 Park Rd., Ilkeston, Derbys DE7 5DA
Tel/Fax: (0115) 932 0643
In association with Redwood Books

To Barry Goostrey

1945 to 1964

One of our mates who was taken early.

Keith Matthewman
In 1960 as a teacher at William Howitt
Secondary Modern School.

FOREWORD

By

His Honour Judge Keith Matthewman, Q.C.

Narvel Annable has managed to do what most authors never could; that is, to make a book about the details of his schooldays a thoroughly enjoyable read.

In his unique style he gives us a history of people and institutions. He gives us his views on education, past and present, and we are treated to a fascinating glimpse of a school-life in the fifties and sixties, complete with all its sorrows and joys.

You do not have to remember those days to enjoy this book: you do not have to be an educationalist to enjoy this book: but if you are in either group, or both, you will enjoy it all the more - and so will your children.

Keith Matthewman

CONTENTS

Introduction

On an iron cold grey day in December 1963, I was trying to hitch a lift southbound on Telegraph Road, Dearborn, Michigan USA. Eventually a large white Chevrolet Impala smoothly floated to my side. The driver took an interest in the English teenager with his thick Derbyshire accent. This man told me that he was a doctor. I was impressed. Some time later I found out that this was not true. His real profession was that of a teacher at the local High School.

Here is a paradox. Yes, I was impressed to meet a respected doctor. A prestigious job with a high salary. But if he had told me the simple truth of being a teacher, he would have gained even **more** esteem and kudos from the young passenger who dreamed of one day becoming a schoolmaster.

A fascination of teachers and education led me to enter the profession. Even now after retirement, that same drive has caused me to go back through my own schooldays analysing and examining the experiences and relationships of 40 years back. Education today is the subject of much heated political debate and it is to be hoped that this book will generate some local interest in Heanor.

This is a sequel to my first book - "Miss Calder's Children" - A Social History of Belper, Biography and Critique on Modern Education, ISBN 0 9530419 0 5. 'Heanor' will follow a similar format to 'Calder', in that some of the critique will be duplicated where appropriate; most chapters tracing the experiences of myself and contemporaries, and the early chapters going back to previous decades as much as living memory will allow. Like the first, this book reflects a desire to recapture a world I once knew and loved, with values which now sometimes seem long lost. We of a certain age have seen a half century of change, not all of which is for the better. The decline of respect for adults and authority is set out and documented in these pages.

For the most part, the following is a history of two schools -Mundy Street Church of England Boys School (1891 to 1958) and Loscoe Road School, which eventually became William Howitt Secondary Modern (1915 to 1960).

My personal experience of these two schools is just a five year span, but from the boyish age of ten years up to the adolescent manly achievement of fifteen years is a huge leap. It seemed like a great age of time, encompassing a journey from the depths of despair to the heights of blissful happiness. Most of the period from September 1958 to July 1960 were the best days of my life, completely unequalled since. These extreme emotions were generated by the violent contrasts of the two very different schools and the sensitivities of childhood.

To me, Mundy Street Boys School was claustrophobic, hateful, cruel, ugly, dark and despairing; whilst William Howitt Secondary Modern School was open, sunny, kind, loving, leafy green and hopeful. In the Howitt days I jumped out of bed in the morning, eager to taste life and cycle to school. At Mundy Street Boys School it was as Shakespeare said in "As You Like It" - *".....the whining school boy....creeping like snail, unwillingly to school."* Every day at Mundy Street was very much a case of the 'Monday morning' blues.

In exploring these two schools I will frequently refer to a third, the large comprehensive where I taught history for the last part of my career (1978 to 1995) at the sharp edge of the chalk face. Contrasting the standards, practices, atmosphere and perspectives of both pupil and teacher in the 1950's and 1990's, on both sides of the Atlantic, should make for interesting reading. As a teacher I carried within myself the idealised models of best practice in the form of - Miss Florence Calder, Mr Peter Crofts, Mr Leonard Smith, Miss Mary McLening, Mr Maurice Brentnall, Mrs Doris Cook and Mrs Maud Buxcey. This book will express a deep sense of disquiet in examining the ever creeping poison of progressive child-centred practice which has undermined the high standards of these excellent teachers.

The story of my comprehensive school is typical of many since the 1960's. The name and town will not be disclosed since this is not a criticism of a school, but rather a 'school of thought'. After seventeen years of service, I have respect and affection for some of my

8

conscientious ex-colleagues and would not wish to hurt them with the expression of sharp philosophical differences.

The Howitt days are remembered with affection by most of its pupils as will be amply demonstrated here in the following pages, and by the annual reunions kindly organised by Brian Brailsford. It was a

magical time of youthful hope and happiness reflected by constant cheer and laughter. The school gates will not limit the depth of this book. I hope to recreate the optimistic social atmosphere of teenagers taking their leisure, enjoying the popular culture of the day, and for the record, to explore the gritty, unpretentious, honest character of Heanor folk.

Brian Brailsford
Thanks to this youth, who we knew as 'Briss',
former pupils of William Howitt Secondary
Modern School enjoy an annual get-together,
forty years on!

The scope of this work will also attempt to include a wider history of the two Heanor schools well before my time, and also after, up to the present day. I am grateful to a number of elderly Heanorians who have given evidence, and shared their anecdotes and experiences to be preserved in the following pages. It has been important to talk to them before it is too late and thus gives this work the authenticity of primary evidence.

Articles in the local press together with a BBC Radio Derby interview have produced a reasonable response from former pupils who came forward with a mixture of memories of life in Heanor, in and out of school. I apologise to those people (of which there must be many) who have been unable to furnish information, because they could not be contacted personally and were never reached by the media or word of mouth.

The following has been verified as far as time and money will allow, but the story of Heanor Schooldays, inevitably will remain incomplete. Even now after publication, I invite readers to contact me with further information or clarifications they may wish to offer, and could be useful in a second edition. I shall be pleased to hear from you.

Contributors to this work have expressed a wide variety of views about the social apartheid created by the 11+ Exam, and this has given me an opportunity to look at the Heanor Grammar School which has its own proud and interesting history.

Mundy Morning Blues

In the year of 1891, on the morning of November 2nd, the newly built Mundy Street Boys School in the very centre of Heanor, opened its doors to 189 boys. Mr Henry Dix the headmaster was the only certificated member of staff. He was one of the well known Dix family of teachers and headteachers from Smalley at that time. John Hibbard was an unqualified assistant teacher. T. Horsley was a third year pupil teacher and W. Granger a first year pupil teacher. Four staff for 189 boys, making an average class size of 47 boys! Two days later a further 85 boys had been added to the books which boosted the class size to **68** boys in each room!

Horsley and Granger, young and inexperienced would have been struggling. They were the brainchild of a man called James Kay - Shuttleworth who in 1839 introduced a 'pupil teacher system'. Mr Richard J. Cootes tells us - *"Starting at the age of thirteen, pupil teachers, were like apprentices who helped the older teachers during the day and studied in their spare time. After five years they took exams to become assistant teachers or qualify for entry to a teacher training college."* Mundy Street, like many schools of the day, had great difficulty getting enough experienced and qualified staff to teach its boys. The 1892 entry in the school log book complains of - *"quite a dearth of teachers"* and pupil teachers were used up to 1905. For five years they earned an annual salary of fifteen pounds, less than 30p or six shillings each week! This was poor pay even by late Victorian standards when they could earn much more in a factory or down a coal mine.

On January 29th 1892, Mundy Street Boys School advertised for a 'Certificated Master' offering a salary of £65 per annum, £1.25 or 25/- per week. The rate for an unqualified 'Assistant Master' was ten pounds a year less. The Mundy Street Boys School log book along these early years also shows other grades as - 'ex-pupil teacher', 'temporary monitor', 'article 33 of code' and 'article 50'. As a comparison it may be interesting to note that 56 years later in 1948 a teacher took home the weekly rate of six pounds. In 1969 leading teaching unions ran a 'spoof' advertisement in the national newspapers, inviting young recruits into the profession. After listing all the many duties and responsibilities, in large print it proclaimed the net pay of a starting teacher - Twelve Pounds per Week! Twenty six years on at the time of my retirement in 1995, my net pay was over £250 per week.

Such is inflation and the varying fortunes of teachers.

When Mundy Street Boys School was just two years old, the number on the books was at its maximum of 400 boys to be dealt with by seven staff. Mr Dix had four unqualified 'assistant teachers' - W. Frost, R. Mellors, G. Priestly and J. Waterfall. W. Granger was by now a 4th year pupil teacher and T. Williamson was a 2nd year pupil teacher.

At this point compulsory attendance had only been introduced 13 years before in 1880. Forcing children to go to school from the age of five to ten brought to light many social problems. A coal mining town like Heanor would have been typical with boys being shown to be dirty, poorly fed, with skin problems, constant running noses, badly shod in ragged clothes and some suffering from infectious diseases. Mr Peter Crofts once commented upon how much more scruffy were the boys in his day as a pupil at Mundy Street Boys School, during the years of 1936 to 1940. In the following decade Pam Carter (of 'Bygones' fame in the Derby Evening Telegraph) recalls certain children who could not come to school in wet weather because they wore cardboard in their shoes to block up holes. Another decade later Horace Hart referred to a friend with a part Quaker Oat box in his shoe!

Back to the Victorian Period and Richard J. Cootes tells us - *"Many School Boards had to arrange for cheap meals, free medical attention and the distribution of charity clothing for the most ragged children. Schools were drab and poorly equipped sometimes having up to ninety pupils in one class. A shortage of trained teachers meant it was necessary to recruit many unqualified assistants and pupil teachers. The curriculum consisted of little more than the bare essentials of reading, writing, arithmetic and Scripture. Elementary education in this period was designed to teach the poor to 'know their duty and keep their place', NOT to help them rise above their station."*

12

1891 was not only the year of completion for Mundy Street Boys School, but also when elementary education was made <u>free</u> for all children. Up to then a small weekly fee had been charged to all families with the exception of the very poor. My own maternal grandfather Thomas Clifton (1880-1963) who would have gone to school in Stanley Common in 1885, said he had to take to school three pence per week.

If it was a hardship making young boys go to school, at least it rescued them from the even worse hardship of labouring in deep dirty dark coal mines. Long hard hours in winter months meant that they hardly ever saw the sun, not to mention the teasing, swearing, fighting and 'belting wit' buckle' from some rough, cruel older miners.

Mundy Street Boys School was built at a cost of £32,000, a massive sum in those days. As a miserable child looking up at the grim north east face of Mundy Street Boys School, I often wondered about the mysterious initials, still visible today carved underneath the coat of arms.   C.E.L.C. and A.E.M.M.
These were the two men who funded the school. The latter being the immensely wealthy last Lord of the Manor who gave his name to the street and school - Alfred Edward Miller Mundy (1849-1920) the Squire of Shipley Hall from 1877. No cardboard in <u>his</u> shoes! His ownership of extensive estates and the local coal mine supported a life in grand style with 25 servants and 30 gardeners, on one occasion giving hospitality to King Edward VII.
Shipley Hall was a splendid home with many spacious rooms, including a ballroom which housed a twenty foot electric German organ and a beautiful cut glass chandelier. The remarkable Glass Corridor and the Conservatory recreated an exotic tropical paradise growing oranges, nectarines, lemons, limes, grapes, peaches, figs and melons. All complemented with a riot of colourful flowers, palms and luxuriant giant ferns with 'beautiful green fronds drooping over the miniature ledges of rock'. To those few humble Heanorians who had the chance to glimpse such opulence, it must have seemed like another world! Particularly for the grimy hard working men directly underneath this glass palace.

The son of the Squire, who gave his name to Godfrey Street, thought better of it and sold the lot after the old Lord died in 1920. After two

13

hundred years of Mundy residence, the great Georgian Hall was slowly sinking and being destroyed by the absence of the very same black rock which funded its original birth - coal. Due to lack of regular maintenance and mining subsidence, the mansion was demolished in 1943. Today you can visit the outline of the site at Shipley Park, a shadow of its former glory, neatly laid out in beautiful gardens and well worth a visit to see the spring rhododendrons.

C.E.L.C. stands for Claud Evelyn Lacey Corfield, who was the Rector of Heanor from 1885 to 1911 when he became the Canon of Southwell. He was the second son and longest serving from a family of successive vicars of the 15c St Lawrence Church situated in Heanor Market Place. Father and three sons gave a total of 51 years service spanning two centuries to the town on the hill. Frederick Corfield 1866-1879 (13 years) and his sons - Conyngham 1879-1886 (7 years) Claud 1886-1911 (25 years) and Ashley 1911-1917 (6 years). I always imagined Canon Claud to be a censorious disapproving Victorian, but he looks a relatively pleasant young man in the 1903 photograph on page 16 of Around Old Heanor.

In a 1923 paper, the second Headmaster of Mundy Street Boys School, Mr Frank Boam speaks very warmly and even regally of Mr Claud Corfield -"...to whose enthusiasm and hard work the school owes its origin. The Rev. Canon Corfield graciously gave his consent for our school badge to be based on his family crest. It seems fitting that one so highly respected by the pupils of the school, past and present, should have by means of the badge, a permanent association with the school."

Mr Boam goes on to explain the meaning of the badge which is a hand grasping a Wreath of Laurels, an ancient Greek symbol of a great prize, a well won honour, the highest place in a competition. In view of my experiences at the school some 32 years later, I found his interpretation of the hand and the heart interesting - but with some personal bitter irony! *The Hand is the sign of true friendship. Friends we make at school are the ones which will have the strongest influence*

14

during later life; hence the Hand as incorporated in our badge, should serve as a reminder of the duty we owe to one another. The Heart is the emblem of love. It is this love which should make us a loyal united school, faithful to ourselves and to our God. Such a spirit will help us in our effort to make ourselves true men."

In the mid 1950's there was no compulsion to wear a school cap, but I fully agree with Mr Boam's 'Special Word to Present Scholars' - *"Remember, at **all** times that the Badge on your cap will mark you as a pupil of our school. The standard of the school will be measured by your conduct: therefore, wherever you are, never do anything which will dishonour the badge you are privileged to wear."*

The Headmaster explains the Corfield and now Mundy Street Boys School Motto - "Serva Fidem" - 'Keep your Trust' or 'Keep your Faith'. *"A fine motto. Every Mundy Street boy or Old Scholar will try to be true to his friend and true to his school and keep the Christian Faith. Without that Faith our life will be a walk in the dark".*
Mundy Street Boys! Be True - SERVA FIDEM!

Alas Mr Boam would be disappointed by some of my utterances in this book about his school, but I can assure him that the memories are clear and very true! One 'old boy' nostalgically broke into the half remembered school song which he suspected was the creation of the headmaster - *"Ye boys, ye boys of Mundy Street ...."* Joe Mee who was there in 1925 tells me these words were set to the tune 'Raise the Flag On High'. Mr Boam received his appointment during the Great War in 1915, but with other members of his staff, he was called up to do battle with the 'evil Kaiser' two years later. A Mr Lane took over until the return of Frank Boam in February 1919.

Mundy Street Boys School Log Book is a very interesting source of information. In September 1893 school attendance was poor due to an epidemic of diphtheria, a pit strike and 'boys being sent to fetch free gifts of bread'. Out of a total of 313 boys, 81 were absent. Many were late for school because they had been having charity meals (breakfast and dinner) at houses of parents who were not on strike, but too far away from Mundy Street.

On September 1st 1893 Mr Dix writes - *"It would be advantageous if the donors of meals would choose more suitable times. I have mentioned the matter to the school attendance officer."*

In the same year the Medical Officer closed the school from January 5th to February 2nd due to an epidemic of measles. Whooping cough, scarlet fever and chicken pox occasionally struck Heanor and closed schools. Influenza closed the school twice in 1918.

Regarding his schooldays Philip Eggleshaw spoke of the - *"...eagerly anticipated Empire Day when all the schoolchildren gathered in the Market Place in the morning, were addressed by the worthies of the town and patriotic songs were sung."*

After that they had the rest of the day off! The above is supported by the log entry for May 22nd, 1907 - *"The boys saluted the flag and sang the 'National Anthem' before assembling in the Market Place with the scholars of Commonside School. There they sang 'Heart of Oak' and the 'National Anthem' and were addressed by the Rector in the presence of over 1000 people."*

The school inspection report of November 1892 was generally favourable - *"The boys are remarkably attentive and display considerable interest in their work. The attainments throughout are of high character with the exception of a weakness in spelling and English of the fourth standard. The singing is very good."*

Twenty years later the Inspector from the Derbyshire Board of Education was more critical of the buildings- *"There is no teacher's room and no office accommodation."* It was to take nearly 60 years before the school would have a staff room and 43 years before the Headmaster had his own private office. *"No classroom is adequately or properly ventilated and several are badly lit. The classrooms are not suitably warmed and temperature records are very low in some rooms. Far greater attention should be given to the daily cleaning and dusting of the school rooms!"* Clearly this was well before the arrival and good work of Victor Beeby and Mrs Whittaker as we shall see later.

In December 1897 it is recorded that the curriculum of Mundy Street Boys School consisted of - arithmetic, algebra, reading, spelling literature, singing, geography, and use of the Prayer Book and instruction in the Catechism. This a question and answer lesson giving boys a brief summary of the basic principles of religion. No mention of games, history or science, but there was an 'Object Lesson Box' which contained samples of items which could be examined by the pupils as they memorised a standard text. The master handed round minerals of, salt, iron, coal and gold. Common objects included leather, coins, a lead pencil, a bell and a clock. Common foods were tea, coffee, water, milk and sugar. Common phenomena were - rain, snow, ice and clouds. Unless stuffed, it must be presumed the following birds to be learned were pictures of - robin, eagle, swan and skylark. Animals - rabbit, cat, horse, sheep, cow and dog. These lists seem strangely arbitrary and short one hundred years later!

In June 1917 too many boys were arriving at school late so all classes were given a moral lesson on - 'The evils of children going to bed late!'

A survey found that more than half the boys went to bed 'late' (after 9.00pm) and a third went to bed 'excessively late' (after 10.00pm). It is written down that an admonitory lecture was given to all the boys on the longest day of June 22nd - when it is quite tempting for them to be playing out in the sun after 10.00pm!

As a result of the 1918 Fisher Education Act, the school leaving age was raised from twelve to fourteen and facilities were provided for physical training (PT) and sports. Consequently the boys of Mundy Street were for the first time, taken to the local swimming baths at Langley Mill and the Local Education Authority granted the school five pounds per annum for the rent of the Heanor Town Ground.

The log book is written in cautious undramatic official tones. It has been interesting to contrast the careful noncommittal language with the colourful outspoken emotional revelations of boys who are now men in their mid 70's. On November 25th 1932 an unnamed female teacher reported an accident – *"A pencil point had been broken in the inside joint of the forefinger of her right hand. The headmaster dressed it with iodine. She had to be taken to hospital because of her finger on December 1st. She did not resume her duties at the school until March*

13th 1933. As a result of her accident she permanently lost the use of the first finger on her right hand."

I discovered that this mistress had the curiously contradictory name of Miss Minnie Large who lived at Langley Mill opposite the cricket ground in Station Road. She taught the youngest class of seven to eight year olds, and was according to one ex-pupil -

> *"Vicious! She stabbed herself because of her habit of stabbing others!"*

Apparently it was her custom to maintain maximum attention by giving unsuspecting boys a sharp poke with the shaft of a pen or pencil, in either the shoulders, neck or head. Her fifteen month absence was the result of one powerful poke too many and too sharp! Due to her injury she was left with a permanent rigid digit, which for many years later was put to good use. She is well remembered as the strict teacher with a stiff finger giving naughty boys a sudden and painful poke.

An HMI Report of 1935 described the school *"..for boys of all ages from seven to fourteen.."* It went on to say - *"..the surface of the playground is dangerously uneven and a wireless set obtained by the headmaster, at his own expense, cannot be used for want of power which managers might easily provide."* Twenty years later, re-chargeable accumulators moved the fascinating clicking and clacking machines of Mr Peter Crofts, and mains power was finally installed in 1956. Some electricity must have been found on January 21st 1936, when - *"..by the diffused means of broadcasting all the boys were able to hear the Proclamation of Edward VIII as their new King at St James Palace, London."*

Little did they know that they would have yet another King before the end of that dramatic year which saw a total of three Kings of England!

Mundy Street Boys School memorabilia is well represented in the education section of Frank Bacon's charming little museum located in the Old Chapel at Heanor Cemetery. In addition to the many photographs and assorted artefacts, note the old treadle operated potter's wheel which will bring back memories to generations of old boys. Mr Bacon, a mine of interesting information, will be only too pleased to make your visit instructive and enjoyable.

A Feared and Frosty February Face

The classes of the 1940's were -

Class 1, Miss Minnie Large who was, I am informed a lady of average size. In the public houses of Heanor, a popular quote makes the rounds about a certain - Jock Brown, who honestly and humorously admitted his limited ability and lack of progress thus - *"I started in Class 1, and bloody well finished in Class 1!"*

Class 2, Miss Holden.

Class 3, Mr Billy Smith who lived on Wysall Street and whose reputation has inspired the title of this chapter.

Class 4, Mr Clarence Redgate who lived on Douglas Avenue and must have been in his late 50's. He is first mentioned on the staff as a second year pupil teacher in 1904!

Class 5, Mr Leslie Thorpe, remembered for his reprimand - *"You blessed wesha woman!"* He was the Deputy Head and took over as the headmaster for a short time when Mr Boam died in 1943.

In 1947 a new popular young pupil teacher called Ernest Pool of Kingsway is mentioned together with Ronald Palfreyman of Mount Street.

The title of this chapter comes from 'Much Ado About Nothing' by William Shakespeare. It was quoted to me by an 'old boy' from Mundy Street called Barry Forster who was at the school from 1941 to 1948.

He said -   *"Billy...you have such a February face,*
                so full of frost, of storm and cloudiness."

Mr Forster was not looking at me. His eyes seemed to be focused on a period nearly 60 years far away down the long passage of time. This line was delivered with a curious intensity of emotion, a mixture of recalled awe, fear and respect. He is the main contributor for this chapter and the next. Also he was the first to mention the infamous teacher - Mr Billy Smith. Other Heanorians now well into their 60's, 70's and 80's would speak of this hard and severe schoolmaster, but some prefer to remain anonymous.

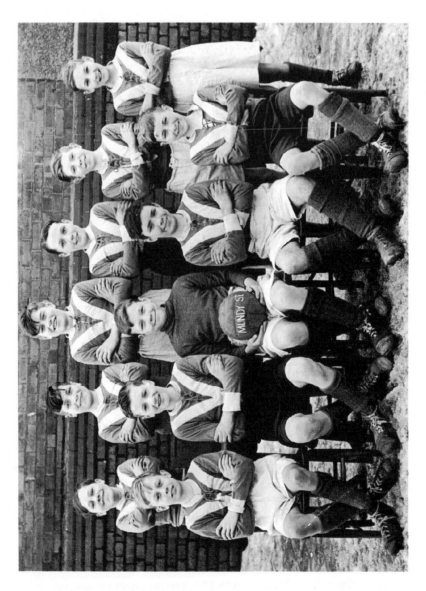

Mundy Street Boys School Football Team 1946

Standing from left to right - Gerald Mozely, Norman Parkin, Barry Smith, George Hemstock, Derek White (Captain) and Donald Purslow. *Seated* - Peter Herrett, George Severn, Peter Mason, John Boyce and Barry Forster.

Mr Forster tells me that the redoubtable Billy, even long after death cast a fearful shadow over the Mundy Street School Centenary Celebrations of 1991. It was well attended with enthusiasm and elderly men were examining old documents with great interest. *"One old chap was looking at the punishment book and seemed nervous. 'I keep looking over my shoulder, and am thinking he's coming through the door now!'"*

That octogenarian would have been taught by a young Billy Smith who is first mentioned in the 1921 staff list - *F. Boam, certified headteacher, M. Hart, uncertified mistress, K. Jarret, uncertified teacher, **W. Smith**, uncertified teacher and A. Benson, uncertified mistress.* William Smith was injured in the First World War, but not by enemy action. He was pierced by a sword during fencing practice which left him without the use of his right arm.

This puts me in mind of the stipulated qualifications of the schoolmaster for Smalley Boys School in 1721 as we learn from Joyce Crofts and Joseph Read in 'Footsteps through Smalley'. *"Apart from being an honest, virtuous and sober man, the Endowment asked that he be able to read, write, cast accounts and the rules of grammar, be literate and have **at least one good arm with which to wield the cane**!"* Billy Smith had just that - one good left arm.

As Barry Forster remembers to his cost - *"When you were called to the front, you knew where the blow was coming from and could be prepared. You were riding it before it came! Not one boy who went through his class escaped without getting at least one good hiding. Poor, or well to do, we all at one time felt the left hand of Billy Smith! Sometimes parents would turn up at the school complaining of excessive punishment. Father went to the school when my brother had his ear smacked which caused a swollen mastoid. During the summer holidays some lads would fret in deadly fear of moving up into his class."*

I am given to understand from some of my comprehensive ex-colleagues that similar distress and 'fretting' befell certain unfortunate pupils who learned in July, that their September destination was to be the class of a certain Mr Annable! Back to Mr Forster - *"Because of Mr Smith's horrendous reputation, they were so miserable, and fretted so much, that some of them left Mundy Street Boys School and went down the hill to Loscoe Road Boys School.*

In the mornings I can remember mothers outside the school holding tomatoes, fruit and cake. These items still on ration were peace offerings for Mr Billy Smith! He was being bribed to go easy on their lad!"
It was the same young Mr Smith who taught and thrashed my old uncle now approaching his 90th year. In desperation he ended up throwing a full ink well at his perceived tyrant!

Joe Mee who was born in 1912 is one of the oldest contributors to the Mundy Street annals in these pages. In general he said - *"They were tough times. God help you if you stepped out of line, but it didn't do us any harm."*

In 1925 at the age of 13, young Joe lived at Stanley Common. Like the author some 33 years later, he made the daily mile walk, from his house to the Rose and Crown bus stop to wait for a bus en route to Heanor. Mine was a happy destination in 1958, but Joe was going into the class of Mr Billy Smith! From an old photograph, and the assumption that Mr Smith started teaching in his early twenties, we can say that he is probably about as old as the century. His injury weighed him down on one side affecting his walk - and unfortunately gave cruel amusement to some of his pupils who dubbed him 'Billy Oddball'. Mr Mee told me of a day when a cleverly done large listing chalk caricature of the slightly deformed master, appeared on one of the doors of Heanor Town Ground. Below was printed - 'Billy Oddball'.

"He was outraged! To our puzzlement, everybody in the class was given a piece of paper and told to draw the character we had all seen and laughed at." After a period of silent sniggering, he carefully examined the artistic labours of love. *'Right! Got you!'* - He cried, and pointed to the boy who had produced the closest match to the original. In a desperate effort to escape sudden vengeful violent retribution, the hapless lad leapt over two desks, but fell and was wedged fast into the gap between the second and third. Thus trapped, the furious teacher thrashed him on the spot. He confessed, but the punishment took its full course as a grim example to others who may be tempted to make fun of an infirmity.

When the Second World War broke out in September 1939 there was a great fear of massive death and destruction rained from German bombers in the sky. Consequently it was decided to take children out of

Class of Mr Billy Smith 1925

Not a single smile! The feared frosty face of Mr Billy Smith was nearby when this photograph was taken of these forty miserable thirteen year olds at Mundy Street Boys School. Joe Mee (fourth from the right second row down) said - *"We were a rough lot, and you can see the terrible poverty. Water toilets were rare. I was one of the lucky few to get into the tin bath once a week, but a lot of the others just stunk!"*

the densely populated areas of big cities, and move them to relatively safe backwaters such as little old Heanor, unlikely to get much Nazi attention. If the boys from Birmingham had any idea what was awaiting them at Mundy Street Boys School, and could have made an informed choice, they may well have chosen Hitler to the tender mercies of Mr Billy Smith!

Mundy Street Boys School was due to open on September 4th 1939. Since there were no air-raid shelters available near the school, it remained closed. Mr Boam wrote in the log book - "...for the time being the children will be safer at home." This pleasant state of affairs was not to last indefinitely. The boys were back on November 20th. No lights were allowed to be visible after sunset, so school opened at 1.20 and closed at 3.30pm. These were the days of double summer time. Mornings were restored the following year, but pupils started at the later time of 9.30 when the bright coal fires did not contravene the black-out regulations. Air raid shelters were dug out in the playground in November 1940. According to the log book, Heanor did get at least one bomb! During the night of 1942, two panes of glass were shattered by the blast.

The alarming events of May 10th 1940 had the sad effect of shortening the Whitsuntide holiday, and also reduced the summer holidays from four to two weeks. The German invasion of Holland and Belgium was seen as a very serious development, and on the same day Mr Neville Chamberlain resigned, and Mr Winston Churchill took over as the new Prime Minister with - "..nothing to offer but blood, toil, tears and sweat." Mundy Street Boys School began to lose teachers in the 'call up' to fight the enemy - but alas not Mr Billy Smith!

He was there with a reduced number of masters to receive the evacuees from Hawshorn Road Junior School in Birmingham on December 4th 1940. Several stories are told of how William Smith tamed these unruly 'tough hard nuts' from the big city. It was said that 'he could lift any lad over two desks'! The principal recollection involves an evacuee called Douglas.

As usual, it was deadly quiet in this stern master's room, in spite of the extra numbers of Brummies. The call of nature caused Douglas to raise his hand - "Please Sir, may I leave the room?" The 'All Powerful' gave a slight nod of assent. In usual procedure, the lad went to the cupboard at the side of Mr Smith's desk to get some toilet paper.

24

Opening the cupboard door, he was in a position to be seen by the other boys - but not the teacher. The temptation was too strong! As to what actually followed next, accounts differ. He used his vantage point to make an unseen rude contemptuous silent 'raspberry' in the direction of the sitting pedagogue and/or gave him an obscene salute.

Douglas had not thought through the effect of his daring conduct upon the intended, and alas thrilled audience - who reacted with amused and delighted expressions. Unfortunately for the young entertainer, such response was seen, and noted by Mr Billy Smith! His furious retribution was violent and swift -

*"He kicked the door of the cupboard which
smashed into Douglas laying him out flat!"*

The other much remembered incident needs to be contrasted to my own experience over a half century later.

I had become well accustomed to the daily run of the mill difficulties in the classroom at my comprehensive school. However it was with shock and horror that I came to be aware that recent generations have been allowed to behave badly in the House of God. Each Christmas, just before the end of term, we attended a Carol Service in the local church. What should have been a pleasant nostalgic occasion each year, I began to dread more and more. Modern educational philosophy makes a big mistake in letting adolescents sit together in friendship groups. The worst types will cling in unison and create the worst possible conduct. They always do. So it was that during singing and even in prayers, there was talking, giggling, nudging, fidgeting, eating sweets and any manner of sacrilege. In outrage I glared over, but it could be seen that senior members of staff were nearer to this blasphemy than myself. They took the easy path and ignored the unignorable.

Mr Billy Smith was part of a past regime and culture which would not tolerate inappropriate behaviour in an assembly of pupils. He was not constrained by fear of physical action, red tape and the delay of reporting bad conduct. He dealt with the few and far between problems immediately and effectively.

In those Mundy Street war years, one big lad was much respected and feared - Masher, so called because he was the 'top dog' and could 'mash' any boy in the school. One morning he was one of the several big youths who stood at the back of Mundy Street Boys School hall, silently facing the headmaster at the front, and overlooked by the other teachers who were standing at the side. On this particular day the customary stillness and respect was slightly impaired by some movement, fidgeting and minor fooling around which drew a sharp irritated comment from Mr Boam. *"Who is causing a disturbance on the back row?"*

And here is the interesting point - <u>all</u> eyes flashed to Mr Billy Smith! As Mr Forster said - *"We all knew what was coming! He was no more than 5', 6", but in these cases it was always Billy who would wade in and give them a thrashing on the spot in front of the whole school!*
He'd been monitoring the group of large lads on the back row, and was now manoeuvring himself, stalking to get a better view of the situation, judging who was most culpable. The culprit was no less than Masher, an unruly adolescent who stood head and shoulders above the schoolmaster. Billy pounced! Got him by the collar, pulled him by one hand through the lines of lads, across the front of the class towards the door - with a few clouts on the way."
Brutal Billy then opened the door and threw out the miserable Masher. When Mr Smith went to close the door - an unusual incident occurred which made this drama remain in the collective Mundy Street Boys School memory. The humiliated, vengeful and maddened Masher, with all his pent up violence and strength - gave the door a mighty kick! This sent Mr Billy Smith reeling and spinning back into the hall. In this brief moment, Masher was a hero -
"We all felt he'd struck a blow for us!"
But that day was the beginning of a vindictive close scrutiny where - *"Billy would never let Masher rest, right up to the day of his leaving school."*
In the playground he would occasionally even climb one of the trees to avoid the unforgetting and unforgiving schoolmaster.
On the whole Masher's reputation suffered - *"It took him down a peg and we didn't think much of him after that."*

Another ex-pupil said - *"William Smith put the fear of God into everybody. You always knew when he was going to attack! His face went absolute scarlet, and his bristles would stick out as if he hadn't shaved. His catch phrase was - '**You confounded idiot!**'"*

Barry Forster remembers the time he had worked hard to learn some poetry. He was confident he would perform well in front of this large class of Heanor boys and the evacuees - BUT.

26

"As I was manoeuvring around the many desks to get to the front, to my horror Mr Billy Smith said - 'Forster! Take that frown off your face!' I simply didn't know how to remove a frown?

So Mr Smith knocked it off!

I never did get to recite my poem, but I wasn't his favourite target, that was Norman in the music lesson. A sort of whipping boy! If anything didn't suit - he'd clout Norman!

With one lad whose father was a local shop owner, he did get it wrong. Giving him a dressing down, he said -

'Holland! You are not fit to clean your father's boots!

This was the same Jimmy Holland who went on to become a GP and later a surgeon. It was a sad loss to Heanor when he died at the age of 58 in the December of 1994."

In spite of this appalling catalogue of beatings, bashings, canings, cloutings and thumpings, not one single contributor would condemn or even criticise Mr Billy Smith! The consensus of opinion is -

"We could do with a few more of his type today!"

This generous attitude is perfectly summed up by Barry Forster -

"In his eagerness for us all to learn, he seemed to trip over tender and compassionate moments. His drive and obsession for discipline had no bounds. He was an old fashioned teacher who taught with a rod of iron with the result that if you didn't know a lot when you went into a class, you could rest assured that this was not the case when you came out!

He believed that literacy was the bed rock of education. Whether poetry or fractions, until you got it right - you were not going home!

As lads, we did lads' things and expected to pay for our wrong doings. He taught us a sharp lesson - and we were all the better for it. Discipline had to be established, and it came in the form of the never to be forgotten - Mr William 'Billy' Smith. Some called him a tyrant, but he influenced and moulded my character. We gained a lot of knowledge, some of it knocked in! We deeply respected and admired this hard disciplinarian who forced us to learn. I would like to see a return of the likes of Mr Smith, but alas, he never will return. Thanks to his old values, all those who came out of Mundy Street Boys School were better citizens."

Mundy Street Boys School Football Team 1947-48

Back row standing - Norman Parkin, Stuart Parkin, Barry Smith, Gerald Holmes, David Morse, Keith Beer and Peter Mason. *Seated* - Barry Forster, George Severn, Derek White, John Boyce and George Hemstock.
On the ground - Gerald Mozely and Malcolm Barton.

War, Winter and Tall Trees

On December 22nd 1939, Mr Boam wrote - *"The boys have given up their Christmas Treat and with the money thus saved, assisted by other little efforts, have sent a Christmas gift to all old scholars serving in His Majesty's Forces."*

It seems that Christmas in the Second World War was a relatively sombre affair, but Barry Forster tells us how they made the best of it - *"We had a raffle draw for a beautiful Christmas cake made and donated by Smiths the bakers of Godfrey Street, whose sons Harry and Stanley attended the school in the 1930's. All classes contributed a play or song, and prizes were given to the boys who had done well, usually a book presented by the headmaster or the vicar."*

Some fifteen years later, thanks to Mr Peter Crofts, I was overjoyed to find myself on the hall stage being presented with a large colourful copy of '20,000 Leagues Under the Sea'. This must have been for effort, as it certainly could not have been earned by academic achievement! In that very public and stressful moment, with hundreds looking on; the vicar had to explain to me the protocol of taking the book from his left hand, with my left hand, and simultaneously shake his right hand with my right hand. Most confusing.

With war rations and restrictive clothing coupons, Mr Forster told me - *"Our mothers were always sitting sewing, darning, mending something for us to go to school in. Jumpers, socks, shirts, Balaclava helmets and 'hand me downs' - it became part of everyday life."* Making old clothes last was summed up by the war time slogan -

'Mend and make do, to save buying new.'

Mr Forster recalls that boys showed good humour and steadfastness during the difficult war years. In the Mundy Street School playground three or four air raid shelters had been dug out, and once or twice a week there was a practice.

"The poster said in bold red letters -

HITLER WILL SEND NO WARNING!

and so we had to lug our gas masks around with us everywhere, every day, all day long, and wear them during the mock air raid.
In cramped uncomfortable conditions we continued with the lesson as best we could."

He tells us that nails, hands, necks and ears were checked by the class teacher, morning and afternoon whilst in lines.

Paper was in short supply and had to be recycled. Depending upon the amount of paper brought in, boys were rewarded with, and proudly sported a cardboard badge proclaiming a certain rank.

Gardeners were encouraged to 'Dig for Victory' and Mundy Street Boys School acquired a plot on Lockton Avenue. Something to look forward to, gardening became a respite from the classroom and incessant learning. Barry Forster - *"Our class, armed with tools but no knowledge, made the maiden expedition to the site. On arrival, Mr Redgate said - 'Well lads, this is it!' Everybody just looked at each other - it could have been a tiger shoot! After a time of toiling among the high weeds, somebody raised his head and said - 'Sir! I think I've found an apple tree!'"*

Hard work was followed by play.

"After a full day at school, I had to do my paper round, followed by another one the next morning - up with my father at 5.30am! He worked at Shipley Pit.
Books on aircraft identification and train spotting were popular. Comic papers were swapped and read with great enthusiasm.
The Hotspur, Boy's Own, Champion, Triumph, Radio Fun, Rover, Wizard, Dandy and the Beano."

These last, on Tuesdays and Thursdays were a great entertainment, comfort and escape for the author a decade later, during a personal dark period at Mundy Street. If Mr Forster has retained any Dandy or Beano annuals in reasonable condition, he will be pleased to know that their current value is in excess of £50.00 per copy!

"We played snobs, five coloured cubed stones which could just be fitted into the hand. They were then tossed. You tried to catch as many as possible on the back of the same hand. 'Blue brick', played with a tennis ball, refers to the line of bricks on the school wall, still there

today about 2'.6" off the ground. Then we played 'skimming on' with fag cards and a game called 'cross bonny'.

Mundy Street School Sports.

OAK HOUSE WINS THE CORFIELD TROPHY.

The boys of the Heanor Mundy St. School held their annual sports on Monday last on the Grammar School Playing Fields, by kind permission of the Governors and Headmaster. The "weather clerk" was on his best behaviour, and a very happy time was spent.

Oak House won the "Corfield" trophy, having scored 23 points. Elm House, a very close second, obtained 22½ points. Ash House registered 21½ points, and Beech House had a total of 17 points. Keen competition was witnessed in all the events.

The judges were the Rev. S. R. Futers, Vicar and Chairman of the Managers; the Rev. S. Cockburn, Correspondent to the Managers; Coun. F. Sisson, one of the Managers; Mr. J. Gregory and Mr. A. Brookes. The Senior Championship medal was won for the second year in succession by Barry Smith, and Anthony Crofts carried off the Junior Championship medal.

A the conclusion of the events the Headmaster, Mr. Leonard Smith, thanked all who had in any way contributed to the success of the day's proceedings; the Grammar School Headmaster and Governors for the loan of the field; the groundsman for his services; the Vicar, Managers and other judges for their work; the staff for its co-operation; and parents and friends for their interest and attendance. He then called upon the Vicar to make the presentations.

Derek White, captain of Oak House received the cup on behalf of his boys and the Vicar congratulated Barry Smith on his second successive championship medal win.

Miss Ellis, who is the donor of the "Ellis" Cricket Cup, then presented the trophy to the captain of Ash House, this year's winners, thus bringing to an end another memorable day in the history of the school.

Results were as follows:—
—100 yards Flat, Seniors: 1 Barry Hartshorn, 2 Barry Smith, 3 George Severn.

80 yards, 10 to 12: 1 Tony Crofts, 2 David Buxton, 3 Ivor Allsopp.

60 yards, under 10; 1 John Weston, 2 Brian Hunt, 3 John Burton.

Potato Race, Seniors: 1 Barry Hartshorn, 2 George Severn, 3 Norman Parkin.

Potato Race, Juniors: 1 Tony Crofts, 2 John Smith, 3 Ronnie Woodroffe.

Sack Race, Seniors: 1 Barry Smith, 2 Barry Hartshorn, 3 Derek White.

Sack Race, Juniors: 1 Richard Draycott, 2 John Smith, 3 Brian Smedley.

Wheelbarrow, Senior: 1 Barry Smith and Roy Gregg, 2 William Hardy and George Severn, 3 Barry Hartshorn and Clarence Smedley.

Wheelbarrow, Junior: 1 Tony Crofts and John Smalley, 2 John Smith and Graham Scarle, 3 Leslie Martin and Kenneth Underwood.

Throwing Cricket Ball: 1 Barry Forster, 2 Barry Smith, 3 Colin Bestwick.

High Jump, Senior: 1 Barry Smith and Stuart Parkin tied for 1st place, 3 Derek White.

High Jump, Junior: 1 Tony Crofts, 2 Graham Scarle, 3 John Burton.

Notice the reference to Tony Crofts born in 1937, the younger brother of Peter Crofts. Mr Anthony Crofts is now a science master at Harrow School.

Best of all were the winter slides. I'll never forget the winter of 1947. Council workers cleared the streets by hand. Lorry loads were dumped on to the Recreation Ground and we had weeks of fun playing on the eight foot mountains of snow."

31

At a time when I was snugly safe and tucked up in my warm pram, several Heanorians have mentioned that dreadful long hard freezing winter.

A little nine year old Pam Carter was returning from her school on Lockton Avenue through the icy dark streets. Dwarfed by the snow piled up on both sides, and losing her orientation in these deep glacial ravines, poor benumbed Pam, an imaginative child, felt she would be lost forever in this now unfamiliar Arctic landscape. In desperation she knocked on the door of a stranger near the church and asked for refuge and help. *"The kind lady within gave me warmth, comfort, a piece of cake and eventually escorted me through the confusing piles of ice and snow back home to Howitt Street."*

During a warmer part of that notable year, a seven year old, down the hill in Aldercar, was thrilled to be presented with his first tricycle. An ambitious child, determined to go far, was so excited with this new found means of independent transport, that he took off! For the next two hours, his alarmed mother, frantic with worry had no idea where he had gone. His father, being an electrician working down the local pit, was spared this trauma. It turned out to be a long triangular journey for this little mite on his tricycle.

His little legs pedalled along Upper Dunstead Road and on through Wood Linkin into Codnor. Turning due south, he trundled along the main road to Loscoe. At such a tender age, his daring and precocious skills of navigation were impressive, but as we shall see later, this was a boy of exceptional ability. At the foot of the hill of Heanor, he went past Loscoe Road School on the right where Miss Westland was about to retire after 31 years as the headmistress. Then came the long struggle up High Street to Red Lion Square. Eventually up to the Market Place with the Heanor Grammar School on the right, which he would have attended four years later, had his parents not moved to Nottingham.

Now comes the easy and good part -
"I particularly remember enjoying the free wheeling down the hill to Langley Mill. I was also aware of being hooted by the occasional lorry and car. I survived to tell the tale which I think would be extremely unlikely if I tried to repeat the outing in today's traffic."

32

Indeed English history would be different today, if this famous son of Heanor had been run over on that day. For this little boy was no less than The Rt. Hon. Kenneth Clarke, QC, MP, the ex-Chancellor of the Exchequer from 1993 to 1997. I am very grateful to Mr Clarke for taking the time and trouble to send me the above and other personal Heanor memories to which I will refer later.

On February 19th 1943 the boys of Mundy Street School lined the path outside St Lawrence's Church to pay their last respects to Mr Frank Boam. For those dwindling numbers of 'old boys', he is recalled as a strict Victorian who, in the interests of discipline, approved of thrashings, many of which he gave personally.

I was intrigued and interested to discover that his successor was regarded as a new light and breath of fresh air! Mrs Winifred Molly Smith told me that Mundy Street Boys School was a *'grim place'* before her husband took over. *'Then it must have been grim indeed!'* - thought this author. Mindful of the responsibility of writing a historical record, and to compensate for my bitter memories around the personality of Mr Leonard Smith, I have conscientiously cast around for positive evidence to give a fair and complete picture of the cold aloof headmaster I describe in Chapter Six.

It was a 38 year old Mr Leonard Smith who began a headship which was to last for the next 27 years. With regards to discipline his approach and attitude was completely different to Mr Boam's.
Barry Forster - *"We couldn't work out Mr Smith! He would know that someone was guilty of a misdeed, and ask about it. The usual response was 'No Sir'. You would get the cane from Mr Boam, but Mr Smith would say -*
'That's quite all right. I believe you. Go and sit down.'
Perhaps it was a test of conscience, but we were not used to such a novel approach. I can only think what a nice time we had with Mr Leonard Smith. Life became much easier with this approachable gentleman who was held in great esteem."

An old photograph looking south west down Godfrey Street towards a newly built Mundy Street Boys School, was taken in the 1890's. The playground was over shadowed by two large tall trees which are shaped like elms. These may be the same trees described by Barry Forster as chestnuts some 40 years later. *"The lads used to 'throw up' at them."*

Don Poundall left Mundy Street Boys School in July 1954, just six months before I started in the January of 1955. The playground had then lost its green gentle kind foliage, and was an uninteresting, flat plain bare treeless hard tarmac desert. In the chapter about William Howitt Secondary Modern School, effectively set in a beautiful garden, I will draw a sharp contrast between the open friendly leafy glades of Miss Mary McLening and the cruel square hard playground of Mr Leonard Smith.

Readers of my first book will know that I condemned the destruction of a giant venerable old tree in the delightful dank garden of Miss Florence Calder, which is now a car park.

It came to me as a surprise that Mundy Street Boys School was once softened by trees and Donald Poundall sadly remembers the day they were cut down. He once fell on one of the stumps and cracked his nose, which in the view of Mr Leonard Smith, required a visit to the hospital for stitches.

"No way! I told him I wasn't going to the hospital. But Mr Smith didn't insist. He took me home so it could be bathed.

He was a great chap and I enjoyed my days at Mundy Street."

FORM S.A. 24.

Derbyshire Education Committee.

SCHOOL LEAVING CERTIFICATE.

This is to certify that *Barry Forster* residing at *133. Ray Stret, Heanor.* was, according to the Registrar's certificate of birth, which has been produced to me, not less than fourteen years of age on the *22nd* day of *Dec.* 194 8 , and, having complied with Section 138 (1) of the Education Act, 1921, is eligible to leave the elementary school.

Date *22nd Dec 1948*   *L Smith*   Head Teacher.
Heanor. Mundy St. C.E. School.

Loscoe Road School

Mundy Street Boys School may look ancient, but it was not the first school in Heanor to be built for working class children. In 1848, 43 years earlier, a Church of England National School was constructed on the north east side of High Street, opposite Morley's factory, a little way down from my home in Red Lion Square. This old school, which was demolished in the 1950's, was referred to by locals as the 'penny school'. For the very poor, it was in fact free. Thomas P Roscoe became the first headmaster, and his wife the first mistress. It was enlarged in 1890 when a Miss Roper was the headmistress who gave her name to Roper Avenue.

I am grateful to the present headteacher Mrs Dawn Payne for allowing me the fascinating experience of studying the Loscoe Road School log books. There was a heading for February 1st 1915 -
"The New Council School, Loscoe Road, Heanor".
Many years later it would be known as 'Howitt', a sweet name which will always conjure up warmth and affection for this author. Arthur Mee said of the distinguished Heanorian, William Howitt - *"With his wife Mary, he was writing books of poetry and novels for nearly 60 years - when there were not so many books to read."*
That time was the first half of the 19th century. William was born into a wealthy Quaker family just below the church on Mansfield Road. The year was 1792, and the handsome solid house was called 'the Dene', sadly demolished in 1935 to make room for more motor cars.

The very same Mr Henry Dix who opened Mundy Street Boys School in 1891, after 24 years of service, now became the headmaster of the new Council Loscoe Road Boys School on April 12th 1915, during the First World War. The log book reveals that he immediately declared his own war on the caretaker!
April 14th - I find that some of the doors have been scratched badly. The caretaker's attention has been drawn to the need for more thorough cleaning and dusting. I have given her a copy of her duties.

35

April 16th - *I have indicated to the caretaker this morning, before she left the premises, the many cases where <u>no</u> dusting of ledges has taken place. A copy of the caretaker's duties has been in one of the classrooms for some weeks I find!*

May 3rd - *The caretaker's dusting is **again** unsatisfactory. I have drawn her attention to it. There is a general lack of thoroughness about it, and so many places missed.*

May 5th - *Mr Robinson, Clerk of Works, called and <u>noted</u> cleaning of the school, and many cases of omitted dusting.*

May 25th - *I have gone over the dusting with the caretaker and pointed out faults **again!***

Loscoe Road School 1916

Centre seated is the headmaster Mr Henry Dix. As yet I have been unable to identify the other teachers, except for the attractive young lady standing on the left whose name at that time was Maud Earnshaw. Forty four years later, she will be better known to generations of Heanorians with a famous name more fitting to her style and formidable reputation!

Whoever threw in the towel first - the redoubtable headmaster, or the poorly paid besieged un-named lady, we shall never know, because the next entry on this subject says -

June 7th - *Mrs Winfield the* **new** *caretaker took up her duties this morning.*
October 27th - *Desks not dusted at all this morning!*
January 1916 - *Our new caretaker Mrs Winfield has done the holiday cleaning well.*

The tone of the log suggests that the Victorian Mr Dix (born around 1860) was strict with all his staff. The school inspector, while taking account of the problems of war, gives a good report on September 9th 1917 - *"The headmaster has not now the advantage of having an assistant master, (Deputy Head?) but his six teachers are rendering such good service that a very satisfactory level of efficiency is being maintained. Discipline throughout is distinctly good. The boys are easily controlled because a desire to make the most of their school life has become an established principle."*

I am most grateful to Mr Eric Wardle for writing down in graphic detail his early memories of Loscoe Road School. Living at 1 Woodend Road in 1931, it was a very short walk via Cottage Garden Lane to the Loscoe Road Infants School. *"Miss Hardy, the headmistress was a tall regal lady with grey hair and long skirts. Another mistress was called Miss Eady. Her father kept a Singer sewing machine shop on Ray Street. There was a Miss Sibley and the top class was taught by a Miss Thorley, a rather large lady with short hair."*
Like the author more than 60 years later, Miss Thorley bicycled to and from school.

In 1934 young Eric moved up to the senior boys school where the change was dramatic and discipline most pronounced. *"The segregation of boys and girls was total and complete. It was like a nunnery! Under the authority of Miss Winifred A Westland, their headmistress, you barely dared to look at them."*
In her very neat hand, Miss Westland wrote the first short modest entry into the log dated March 1st 1917 -

> *"Have commenced duties this morning*
> *as Head Mistress of this department."*

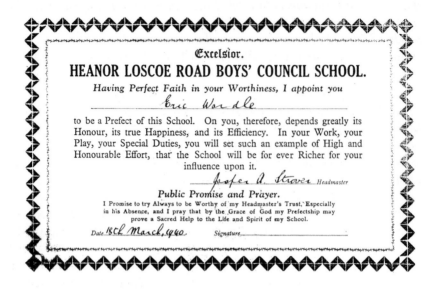

Excelsior.

HEANOR LOSCOE ROAD BOYS' COUNCIL SCHOOL.

Having Perfect Faith in your Worthiness, I appoint you

Eric Wardle

to be a Prefect of this School. On you, therefore, depends greatly its Honour, its true Happiness, and its Efficiency. In your Work, your Play, your Special Duties, you will set such an example of High and Honourable Effort, that the School will be for ever Richer for your influence upon it.

Joseph A. Strover Headmaster

Public Promise and Prayer.

I Promise to try Always to be Worthy of my Headmaster's Trust, Especially in his Absence, and I pray that by the Grace of God my Prefectship may prove a Sacred Help to the Life and Spirit of my School.

Date 18th March, 1940.   Signature

This was the first day of a 31 year appointment which lasted up to the arrival of Miss Mary McLening in January 1948.

In 1921, Mr Henry Dix retired from the Loscoe Road Boys School and Mr Charles Mettam, his successor received a glowing report, in the stilted language of the day from the school inspector on May 12th 1924. *"We consider that Mr Mettam and his assistants are worthy of every praise for fostering the spirit of chivalry and idealism, which spirit is reflected in the unique election for the honour of being the 'Gentleman of the School'."*

Eric Wardle tells me that his headmaster Charles Mettam was feared by pupils <u>and</u> staff.
"A visit to his study up a flight of narrow stairs was dreaded. He enjoyed caning with relish! Six strokes across the hands were readily administered."

For those who had the presence of mind,
his office was a sight to behold.

"Gleaming cups, impressive shields, commendations won by the football team and choir were proudly displayed right round the room. These two subjects featured very highly in the life of the school and much time and effort was given over to them. Miss Robinson was in

charge of the large boys choir, and the headmaster's daughter was the piano accompanist. They gave freely of their time, much of it after school.

Miss Mettam eventually became Mrs Frank Turner when she married the good, but short tempered woodwork teacher. In the well equipped room, his instructions were carried out to the letter, or a boy would get a sound clip round the ear from, as we called him 'Tanky Turner'!

At my last comprehensive school, a similar clip in the Technical Department produced the most appalling row fomented by one persistent angry mother and her disruptive, vengeful son determined to assert his rights. How times have changed!

In 1958 I recall digging in the garden plots under the supervision of Mr Maurice Brentnall at the top of Holmes Street to the west of the school, now a smooth attractive lawn. In the 1930's they were between the girls school at the south end and the rear of the houses in John Street. In my time, as today, it is a pleasant verdant area dominated by the huge lime tree, even lovelier after a further 40 years of growth.

Under Mr Turner's instruction, the ground was divided up into small plots, each to be cultivated by two lads.

"An enjoyable lesson which has helped me in later life. Back in the classroom there was much writing to be done about growing vegetables."

In 1939 the carefully tended plots had to make way for air raid shelters, but digging and growing continued in the large overgrown garden of the empty and spooky Calladine House, which stood near the school at the top of Cottage Garden Lane. This 19th century house was the Heanor Isolation Hospital up to the 1920's, and finally demolished in the 1950's.

Mr Turner also took the boys to Langley Baths where they froze, as we of William Howitt Secondary Modern School froze, a quarter of a century later. (See Chapter 15.) At least we were chauffeured the one and a half miles to the icy waters in buses. Young Eric and his pals had to walk. *"A column of boys, with towels and costumes tucked under arms, would trudge up High Street, across the Market Place, down by Heanor Church into Hands Road, and on to the unheated open air baths opposite Langley Colliery. Heaven help anyone who got out of line or strayed in any way! We changed in small cabins two to a box.*

After 45 minutes tuition, we were ordered out, quick dry, dress and a brisk march back to school."

These primitive pools of murky waters were constructed on the site of a water works in 1910, the very same year as the completion of the heated indoor Belper Baths.

In the early 1950's, Pam Carter spent most of her time swimming in the *"pea green water"*. Perhaps it should be spelt 'pee' in view of Derek Goostrey's assertion that if nature called, nobody bothered to get out! *"We tiddled to kill the frogs!"*

Pam tells me that the price was the same in her day as mine a decade later. *"Sixpence in the posh changing rooms and only tuppence in the grotty ones. Regular lads knew about the knot peep holes, but we sharp girls on the other side who nearly lived at the baths, soon put a stop to that with a hanging towel!"* She and her friends had an equally effective way of dealing with the cold - *"Some days we'd get blue with cold, but Mr Stanway the attendant was a good sort who occasionally would let a privileged few warm themselves in the boiler house. Just up a little incline at the back. It was really lovely, a great treat."*

I remember this man. He was much more pleasant and friendly than his bad tempered and strict opposite number at Gibfield Lane, Belper who once shouted at me and the Goostrey brothers -

"Get out - and doown't come back!!"

No doubt we had infringed one of the many rules boldly proclaimed on wooden boards around the white tiled walls.

Pam learned to swim at the Langley Baths when she was 13. *"Having mastered it at long last, I was so proud that I dragged my father there to watch me. He stood impassive as I struggled, splashed, thrashed and flailed around in a soup of floating beetles and leaves, swallowing half the bath on the way! Great deflation and disappointment when all he said was - 'Now learn the back stroke'. Born in 1910, out of a different generation, he didn't believe in praise which might make you big headed."*

Perhaps every school in pre-progressive days had its 'Billy Smith'. Meet Mr Jeffery. According to Mr Wardle - *"A remarkable teacher who would not stand any form of indiscipline. He kept up to six canes in his cupboard, selecting the one which made the loudest swish on its decent."*

John Wright who attended Loscoe Road Boys School from 1940 to 1947 corroborates this severe reputation. *"Due to a prominent nose we called him 'Beaky Boy'. The worse teacher of the lot, very very very strict. Two of his favourite canes were called 'Big Ben' and 'Little Bertha'. You were given a choice!"*

At the end of this century we have come to the sorry state of many progressive teachers, keen to court popularity with imaginative lesson plans, but alas with no discipline, no order and therefore no work done! Mr Jeffery is a joy to behold. It seems here we have all the elements of an excellent teacher. Eric Wardle - *"He was the one teacher for whom I have the highest regard. This confirmed bachelor gave his all to the profession. A brilliant ornithologist, super musician, together with an extensive knowledge on most subjects, and enthusiasm to impart that knowledge. If you were prepared to work hard in his class, he would readily acknowledge your efforts with lots of encouragement.*
Thanks to Mr Jeffery I saw the interior of a cinema for the very first time and enjoyed the magic of the big screen. He took a party of about ten boys to the Derby Gaumont on London Road to see a film with some educational content. All this funded out of his own pocket including the bus fare from Heanor to Derby."

At that time back in the 1930's, having established his authority in the classroom, the boys would have sat politely and quietly on that bus, and in that cinema. Other members of the public would have been respected at all times. It was the kind of school trip which could only be dreamed about by the dwindling number of traditional teachers in these late 1990's.

The name 'Beaky Boy' may have been connected to Mr Jeffery's love of birds, and a surprising discovery made by John Wright in recent years. *"We were fascinated by a stuffed owl which was always displayed in his classroom. Decades later when Mr Jeffery and his dusty owl were miles, and years away from my mind; at work, I had occasion to go into the caretaker's room at the Herbert Strutt School in Belper.*

There it was. That <u>same</u> old owl - even dustier than ever!

Mr Jeffery eventually left Loscoe Road School to take up an appointment at Belper. Having a great love of birds, he would play records of bird song on his small portable wind-up gramophone, teaching the boys to be able to identify different species.

Loscoe Road School Football Team 1947-48

Roy Palmer tells me that the 'Bucket Bangers' were the 'best school team ever'. *Three teachers standing at the back* - Mr Maurice Brentnall, Mr Jasper Augustus Strover (the headmaster) and Mr Foinette. *Back row standing* - Derek Rowe, Keith Williams, Clarence Harvey, Jack Saxton and Keith Rowley. *Front row seated* - Ronald Gillott, Roy Palmer, Ralph Evans, Colin Webster, Lawrence Harvey and Peter Richardson.

The Loscoe Road Boys School log book gives further details on April 4th 1938 in the bold hand of Mr Strover -
"Mr LK Jeffery commenced work at the school."
"August 29th 1941 - Mr Jeffrey ceased duty at this school having been appointed to a position at a Derby Borough School.
September 1st 1941 - Mr Jeffrey, having visited his new school, has with the consent of the Derbyshire Education Committee, decided to seek re-appointment here."

On April 5th 1937, another bachelor made a big difference to the life and quality of Loscoe Road Boys School. A new headmaster rejoicing in the exulted name of - Jasper Augustus Strover!

A very different personality to Mr Mettam. The approachable and religious Mr Strover had come from his previous post in Hathersage bringing to Heanor - energy, enthusiasm and plenty of new ideas. He was anxious to improve the school's academic performance and at the same time maintaining interest in football, choir, cycling, gardening and motor mechanics. Eric Wardle remembers one morning in particular - *"He drove an old bull nosed Morris car into the playground and parked it next to the woodwork shop. At a time when cars were uncommon, we lads were thrilled to see this two seater with hood and 'dickey' seat at the rear."*

Mr Wardle now suspects that the bouncy vivacious newcomer had purchased this educational resource out of his own pocket. He addressed the curious gathering - *"Now lads! You are going to explore and learn the mysteries of the internal combustion engine by stripping, and then rebuilding all the parts of this car!"*

The inspectors were also impressed with the man of new ideas. Here is part of the March 19th 1938 report - *"The present headmaster has been in charge less than a year and has already brought new life, vigour and system into every part of the school. In all classes the boys give full attention to their work. They are courteous and responsive to their teachers. They show commendable respect for their personal attendance. The headmaster's grip of the situation is evident in that he is conscious of the weaknesses which still exist. There is a need to strengthen some of the fundamentals."*

It was great fun talking to the amusing and entertaining Roy Palmer who was at Loscoe Road School from 1941 to 1948. He also remembers Jasper Augustus Strover. *"I only had the cane off him four times. Not a bad record! He had a big stick with a knob at the end and a smaller stick. **'Which one would you like?'** I tried them both. One day me and my mate Arthur got caught pinching some bantams from a back yard a few houses down. Arthur's dad had a bit of ground with a few pigs and a few fowls. We thought he could do with a few more!"*

Mr Strover took a different view - *"I have to laugh at some of the things you do Palmer, but this is ridiculous! **Which one would you like?"***

But keeping livestock did interest the headmaster. In the school garden area, Eric Wardle remembers pens of pheasants, cute little chicks, and also pens of ferrets.

"I'll never forget Mr Strover, a lovely gentleman
of great integrity who I admired."

Since I had such a rough time at Mundy Street Boys School, it is ironic that they were considered as soft by Loscoe Roaders who referred to them as 'dummy suckers'. John March attended Loscoe Road Boys School in the 1950's and proudly told me that he was one of the 'Bucket Bangers'. Indeed, Roy Palmer's football team had the same title.

In the late 1950's, my fellow pupil Carol Bestwick was enjoying her regular few moments of power and importance, enthusiastically and conscientiously clanging an old hand bell to proclaim the beginning or end of lessons. The bell of the 1930's was more interesting, and possibly even louder than the mighty efforts of Carol. It was part of an aircraft engine cylinder with air cooling fins on the outside. When struck on the inside a strident signal reverberated around the whole campus.

As we shall see later at Mundy Street and the Heanor Grammar School, most pupils are able to recall a teacher who presided over chaos and had no control. At Loscoe Road School there was such a master -

"You could just do what you wanted!"

These people were few and far between. Most of the teachers were out of the mould of Mr Foinette - *"Ay were a bogga!"* His principal means of discipline was the pipe in his top pocket. Roy Palmer -

"He'd suddenly get it out and give you a sharp whack
over the head. He broke three of them on me!"

If the pipe supply ran out, Mr Foinette could always turn to his alternative form of punishment - electrocution!

"He had this gadget under his desk. You held a wire in each hand. It wasn't too bad to start with, but then he would turn up the power and watch you start to shake."

Mr Palmer clearly remembers a growing evil sadistic leer on his master's face, as the power was increased to see how much the culprit could take! In mitigation to Mr Foinette, it would seem that the victim could choose to end his ordeal at will, and the boys would no doubt have enjoyed the entertainment value, and grim novelty of this unusual alternative to the stick.

The log first refers to CJ Foinette in June 1947. On December 21st 1950 it said - *"CJ Foinette concluded his duties here to take up a post under the Leicestershire Authority."*

The staff list for September 1952 shows large classes -
Mr Maurice Brentnall - 37 boys. Mr Chambers - 45 boys. Mr Earnest Allan Priestley - 40 boys. Mr Thorpe - 49 boys. The other teachers where - Mr Arnott, Mr Bessingham, Mr Davies, Mr Goff, Mr Green and Mr Twigg. A total of ten masters for 409 boys.

Mr Priestley, a good teacher first mentioned in 1936, was still there, kindly encouraging me to improve my very poor English in 1960. For some reason he was referred to as 'Nobby Priestley'.

In this atmosphere of harsh discipline, I was interested to hear about the young and inexperienced Mr Maurice Brentnall. At William Howitt Secondary Modern School a quarter of a century later he was the epitome of a mature, kind, highly respected, confident, much loved schoolmaster who could, if need be, cower a class with just a look. Accordingly it was a surprise to hear from Roy Palmer that -*"He was a bit handy with the cane, and it wasn't just a tap! He was keen and did his job. I had it several times, but probably deserved it.*
You respected your teachers in those days."

It has been very difficult finding information about Mr Maurice Brentnall. Most people said - *"I don't remember hearing or reading about his death!"* Based on photographs, I estimate he was born around 1904, and if the 94 year old Mr Brentnall is reading this - please do contact me! The first mention of the venerable master in the log book occurs on September 21st 1927 -
"Mr Maurice Brentnall, student teacher, left
today to enter Cheltenham Training College."
This was in the somewhat difficult hand of Charles Mettam. It is interesting to note that another excellent Heanorian teacher trained at Cheltenham College twenty years later - Mr Peter Raymond Crofts.

Mr Strover showed care and compassion when he wrote -
"Mr Brentnall ill, so I sent him to see the doctor this morning.
18.6.37 - Mr Brentnall gone to Nottingham
General Hospital and is absent from duties."

Jasper A Strover may have been ill on July 14th 1941 when Mr Maurice Brentnall himself was writing the log in an exquisitely well formed style. After the signature he added 'Acting Headmaster'.
The following incident has similarities with the one described 18 years later in Chapter 11. *"On returning to school at 1.20pm, I found that a boy, Hector Meads, in attempting to jump from a window ledge in a cloakroom, to swing on a overhead heating pipe, had fallen on the back of his head and was unconscious. Seeing the boy's condition, I went for Dr Donegan immediately and on his advice took the boy by car to the hospital where he was put to bed. Dr Donegan examined him. He said the boy was suffering from severe concussion, but swelling prevented further diagnosis."*
No further reference to poor Hector.

The log of August 1955 first mentions Mr Morgan Green, remembered for his enthusiastic field trips some as far off as Scotland. Michael Hogg told me about his canoeing adventures. It is in Mr Green's class of 3A that I recognise names which will make a big difference to my life a few years on. Horace Hart was in there, and so was Derek Goostrey who sitting with his friend Joe, together kept a pet white mouse in his desk without the knowledge or consent of Mr Green!

I made a pilgrimage with Mr Eric Wardle to our old school in October 1997. An emotional and nostalgic moment as we walked up John Street and turned right into Holmes Street. The prosperous Heanorian grocer John Holmes began his long life in the reign of George III, and lived through a total of six monarchs to his death in 1919 at the age of 99! His business was at the top of Derby Road. In the 1910 photograph on page 27 of the 'Around Old Heanor' book, the stern bearded and formally dressed Mr Holmes is seen brandishing his finger at a police officer, and seems to be asserting his considerable authority.

Approaching the school, my first impression was rather similar to the first impressions of nearly forty years before - a welcoming green and pleasant campus. Eric shared the same experience, but his was a gap of 66 years since he first attended the infants school. As a 13 year old, I would not have taken direct note of the delightful, nicely tiled, dual raked roofs - gentle and then steeper. I did not particularly notice the generous windows, but all these comfortable architectural features set in a lovely garden, strongly struck a happy positive note after the hard sharp edges of the Dickensian school up the hill.

We walked up towards Cottage Gardens, with the school on our right, and an open green area on our left which was allotments in past days. Leaving the girls section, we passed the one time strict divide and came to the area of the boys. The old cloak rooms seemed to be unchanged and Eric pointed out the stoke hole once used for fuel delivery. These 80 year old buildings are still in excellent condition. At the most northerly tip of the campus we turned right at the class room of the young Mr Maurice Brentnall. Further along we could see the old green house style woodwork room, with its many small panes on three sides, still looking like new. For Eric this was the domain of Mr Turner, but for my generation it will always be the room of dear old Mr Ferraby; notwithstanding the fact that it is now full of books! East of the Infants School, we seemed to be looking into a neglected, but enchanting secret garden of an old overgrown orchard. This turns out to be the old boyhood scrumping ground for Horace Hart and his friends.

"It was like an Aladdin's Cave! Apples, pears and 'goosgogs'.
So handy, right next to the school!

Coming out onto the bottom of High Street, a few steps took us to the foot of Allandale Road. Here there is a dead straight, one third of a mile clear view, all the way up to Red Lion Square and the frontage of the once tobacconist and confectioners of Buckberry's; behind which I spent the darkest and most miserable days of my life. See Chapter 8.

But on Allandale Road the sun was always shining, for this was the happy entrance to the kind class of Mrs Doris Cook, set in the 'Camelot' atmosphere presided over by the wonderful Miss Mary McLening; where after that dreadful period I found hope and joy. The young beech trees, whose lime green leaves during the springtime would seem to glow - are sadly gone, but Allandale House still stands proud and handsome in a lush glade on the right. John Holmes's beautiful gothic home is clearly dated 1884 together with his ornate initials. The impressive steep roofs and tall chimneys are complemented by decorative fascia boards. 'Allan' was the maiden name of his wife.

At the top of this cul-de-sac is the nostalgic east gate of Howitt School and the canteen which features at the very end of this book. This and the other prefabricated buildings did not exist in the time of Eric Wardle. Accordingly he was not to realise the significance of the very first prefabricated classroom we encountered on the left as we entered the school. An emotional experience and shrine which I describe in Chapter 13. Miss McLening, in one of her characteristic short concise entries, refers to these structures in the log on November 30th 1948 -
"The new block of classrooms and homecraft centre were open to parents and friends from 3.00 to 4.00 this afternoon. Work done during the term was displayed for inspection."

Cooking lessons for boys were unusual in those days, but would on a practical level have served me better in later life than the Mundy Street pottery classes. Derek Goostrey tells me he gave a piece of his Christmas cake to Miss McLening - *'grovelling'*. After a taste she said - *"It was lovely!"*

Into the school we are in a lovely leafy glade of the mighty lime tree and an equally splendid copper beech. More large trees grace the tennis court area. Fortunate are the pupils of Howitt, past and present.
The headteacher Mrs Dawn Payne kindly showed us round our old school. We noticed that the whole place was completely clear of any offending sweet papers, empty cans etc. Inside were the very same old lift lid desks which I, and even Eric remembered! Old and worn with normal wear and tear, but in excellent condition after perhaps up to 60 years! No sign of the vandalism of deliberate graffiti so common today. This is a compliment and tribute to Mrs Payne and her vigilant staff, who have worked very hard to get modern pupils to put litter in the correct place, as I know to my cost. At my last comprehensive school, the history staff room kettle sat by a window overlooking a busy entrance to the campus. During tea making it was frequently necessary to bang on the window and reprimand a litter lout, even though it made me very unpopular. The spirit of Mrs Buxcey lived on in Mr Annable!

48

With hundreds of busy children in and out each day, schools are potentially dirty dusty places, but at Howitt my finger did not find a trace of dust. Praise to the hard labour and organisation of Mr John Shepherd the Head Caretaker and his conscientious cleaners.

In one room Eric noticed a cupboard in which canes were once kept, but he looked in vain for the old aircraft cylinder bell. The most rewarding room was the office of the headteacher where we admired the plain and simple stout Victorian desk once used by Miss Mary McLening. Eric drew my attention to the fire grate which was roaring on cold days in the time of Mr Mettam. Four book ends were inscribed -

> *'M. McLening Trophy - Awarded for contribution*
> *to the life of William Howitt Junior School'.*

The most prominent item was a large impressive silver cup for schoolboy soccer, inscribed -

> *"Jubilee Year 1935. The Gregg VC Trophy, presented by the*
> *British Legion, Heanor Branch and Friends to perpetuate*
> *the name and deeds of Sergeant W Gregg VC. DCM. MM."*

War hero William Gregg was born on Tag Hill in 1890, and attended the relatively new Mundy Street Boys School. Becoming a sergeant in the First World War, he was described as -'*..a fighting man his comrades would follow anywhere.'* He was awarded the Victoria Cross personally from King George V in 1918 for - *"Most conspicuous bravery and brilliant leadership in action, which involved the taking of a German machine gun post after twice being forced back"*.

Sergeant Gregg who died in 1969, was a miner before and after his army service. He is also remembered by Gregg Avenue and the new swimming baths.

Coming back to school after so many years had been a moving experience, but now it was time to leave and we thanked Mrs Payne for her courtesy and time. We had come on to the premises of William Howitt Junior Community School at the end of the day as the pupils were leaving. Their conduct can tell much about the atmosphere and standard of behaviour which reflects on the teachers and headteacher. No screaming, jostling or bad language. The evacuation was orderly at a reasonable sound level. All this left a first class impression of the school in which we had been very proud and happy.

Mundy Street Boys School, January 1953.

Evidence that at least one of the tall trees was still standing behind Mr Leonard Smith the headmaster on the right. On the extreme left is the teacher Mr Peter Crofts with his class of 40 boys.

The back row standing from left to right - Trevor Cauldwell, John Richards, Brian Smith, Tony Rue, Brian Smalley, Saxton Kemp, John Ratcliffe, Michael Bryan, Trevor Clarke and Bobby Fowkes.

Next row down standing - Michael Crook, Graham Bullock, Peter Birks, Alan Parks, Tony Burton, Kevin Holmes, Douglas Buxton, Barry Saxton, Keith Hutsby and John Thompson.

Seated - Donald Poundall, Roy Mann, Roger Neal, Terry Beer, Graham Hibbert, John Bullock, Derek Knighton, Arthur Flinders, Christopher Ward and John Smith.

Seated front row - Michael Parkin, Geoffrey Bestwick, Kenneth Driver, Derek Pacey, George Bonsall, Albert Grime, Pat Baldwin, Michael Cope, Colin Calladine and Keith Brown.

Gas Lighting and Open Coal Fires

For the most part the years at this Church of England Junior School were an unhappy period of my life. Overall it was grim and yet at the same time - interesting. One has the impression that in the mid 1950's, Mundy Street Boys School was locked into a pre-war time warp at about the mid 1930's. It was a dingy Victorian building with a Dickensian forbidding atmosphere.

I perceived the headmaster, Mr Leonard Smith as a strict religious autocrat who shaped my early, and I fear, negative attitude to the Church. In this merciless, theocratic, macho all male regime, I was regularly bullied. Why I should want to re-visit these dark years is probably a conundrum for a psychologist. The reader must draw his/her own conclusions, but the amateur historian part of me is keen to write for the record and give credit where it is due.

In re-telling some of the more excruciating moments of this harrowing part of my life, it has been necessary to be deliberately vague about the identity of certain people. The aim is to present to the reader an accurate factual historical account, and yet at the same time avoid upsetting and hurting some Heanorians whose deeds are now approaching a half century into the past. The overall tone and mood of this book is set in the second part - joy and happiness of Howitt.

"Accurate and factual" may bring a wry smile to some faces. No history is ever entirely impartial, unless it becomes exceedingly dull! To cut down on bias, it will be seen in the following pages that I have taken evidence from many witnesses in order to give as wider perspective as is possible.

It was sometime before Christmas 1954 that we moved from Belper to Heanor. I was nine years old. A frail eighty year old Sir Winston Churchill was the Prime Minister who retired the following April in favour of Sir Anthony Eden who called and won the General Election in May.

'Heanor' was just a name, a place somewhere else. It was later that I gradually became aware of the difference in atmosphere and environment. Belper is an old mill town with beauty and charm. It has the River Derwent, meadows, nooks, crannies and cobbled alleys. A fascinating playground for a little boy. Heanor the hill town was harder, more urban with a certain grimness to match my change of fortune. Its reputation was summed up by an overheard comment made by a disappointed visitor to the North Wales resort of Pwllheli, when he dubbed it - *"Heanor by the sea!"*

It was not the best of times for my parents whose shop selling ladies clothes (C&S Outerwear) had gone bankrupt in Belper. Presumably they opened the new shop "Annabel" at 33 Market Street in the name of my mother. It was situated directly opposite Woolworth's. This small shop selling hats, handbags and cheap jewellery had an excellent first day. We took £20.00. Alas that was the last good day. They struggled on until early 1958 when the business failed. On a few occasions, not a single customer came into the shop all day!

Against this background of worry and tension, my problems at Mundy Street Boys School took a back seat. There were two flats above the shop. We occupied the top one which had just three rooms. The lady in the flat below was Mrs Ethyl Boon, affectionately addressed as 'Mrs'. She was an informal part time nanny / housekeeper, a successor to Mrs Marjorie Harrison in Belper. My parents were frequently engaged in either business or social activities.

I still have all but one of my school reports, revealing that I had five main class teachers in the four years from January 1955 to July 1958. The school had other permanent class teachers who occasionally 'took us' and in addition, from time to time, different temporary staff came and went.

At the age of 11, from September to December 1956, a Mr RM Dunn taught our class in the eastern end (nearest Godfrey Street) of the School Hall which runs parallel to Mundy Street. At the leaving ceremony of Mr Dunn, the headmaster surprised us by saying that our departing teacher was over qualified for his job.

"He has a PhD., and we <u>should</u> have been
addressing him as 'Doctor' Dunn!

I was very impressed. A sad loss at the departure of RM Dunn, a good teacher and a gentleman. He had us draw country houses and made me aware of the rich cultural heritage of Derbyshire. My ebbing confidence was boosted when he invited me to bring photographs to school of my sister's honeymoon in America. Sparkling images of a smart beautiful girl on skis in the bright sunshine of Northern Michigan together with several languid poses against an impossibly large impressive gleaming Buick. I preened with pride as he took a kind interest in an exotic setting a million miles from the grimy greyness of Heanor, and commented to another member of staff - *"Coloured photography is very expensive."*

A young Mr Tooher struggled with us in the same room for a short period in 1957. An inexperienced teacher who did not get an easy ride from us. We have all been there! I think it was a Mrs James one of the few females, and strict Welsh lady who taught music. Mrs Tutt was distinctive having an unfortunate grotesque swelling, caused we were told by the local water. It was called 'Derbyshire Neck'. During the Asian 'Flu epidemic of September 1957, a Mr Nicholls filled in for staff illness. He was a patient, gentle and encouraging man. I was remarkably healthy in those days and felt miffed to be one of the few in the whole class deprived of a fortnight off school! Mr Nicholls has kindly loaned me some fascinating old artefacts from the Mundy Street years. Schemes of work, exercise books, class records, handwriting practice sheets and sample questions for the eleven plus examination of 1957. It all came back!

In such a bleak period, Mr Peter Raymond Crofts stands out as an anomaly. Indeed the following will read like a handbook of 'Best Teaching Practice'. My report from Junior 3 dated July 1955 is signed by PR Crofts. It is ironic that forty three years later in 1998, I now write *his* report.

In Robert Bolt's play "A Man for All Seasons" (1960), Sir Thomas More (1477-1535), the famous scholar, statesman and saint, received a visit from a young man called Richard Rich. He asked for a well paid influential government position. In short, a good job. The wise Sir Thomas saw character defects in the ambitious Richard and strongly advised a different course. *"Be a teacher."* After listening to several remonstrations, More stood his ground and insisted - *"Become a teacher."* Rich persisted saying that there was no honour, prestige or money in such a humble profession.

"I'll not be remembered, and who would know if I was any good?" More's reply was very significant -

*"Be a good teacher. Your pupils will know you are good
and will always remember you."*

I remember Mr Crofts. He was good.

It was January 1955 when I started my new school. I was put into Junior 3, a class of 46 boys taught by Mr Crofts in the south western wing nearest to Ray Street. He graciously welcomed me and said - *"Sit with Trevor Wilson."* This was to be a mixed blessing. After being accustomed to the electric lights at my previous school, Long Row Big Boys at Belper, it was intriguing to see the soft gentle incandescence of the gas mantle, operated by the teacher with chains pulled on or off. The pipe and radiator central heating at Long Row gave way to the large open fires at Mundy Street. Mr Crofts recalls pleasant moments on a cold winter's afternoon, when the class was quiet and all that could be heard was the soothing hiss of the lights and the warm friendly crackling fire. He paid tribute to his faithful, reliable and enthusiastic coal monitor, Victor Beeby. The fires were frequently well banked up, soon to be even bigger and more roaring, much to the disapproval of the headmaster, Mr Smith who would occasionally observe and "tut-tut".

It was most inconvenient that Mundy Street was not on the mains as Mr Crofts needed electricity for his home made educational and fascinating machines, well ahead of their time. Power from accumulators fed the clicking, winding, humming and whirling noises. One was a table tester, which by means of illuminated numbers, asked the player the sum of two numbers multiplied. If the correct answer was selected, another similar question was instantly asked. After ten correct answers, the player would be automatically rewarded with a 'spangle', a popular sweet of the day. In this very interesting classroom, I can recall other colourful inviting contraptions with backgrounds cleverly drawn and painted by Mrs Joyce Crofts. One was on the subject of road safety with a vivid zebra crossing and another had large musical notes, but my favourite was the electric shock device. It must

54

have been similar to the aforementioned contraption of Mr Foinette, ten years before and down the hill, but voluntary and entirely for amusement. On my first experience I cautiously set the lowest voltage and complained to onlookers that I could feel nothing. Big mistake! A boy turned it up a few notches, but without any noticeable result. As my small audience grew impatient, one bright spark moved the controls to the very highest setting; when I all but lit up! I am grateful that Mr Crofts had calculated that the maximum current was less than fatal.

One morning we arrived to find a large glass fronted cage designed to display a busy community of white mice, chasing through tubes and treading spinning mills. It was delightful and exciting. We were asked to identify individuals with names beginning with 'M'.
At a later date, three boys made Mr Crofts more angry than we had ever seen him before. 'A' pushed 'B' who fell into 'C' who broke the main front pane of glass. This was established by a serious and sombre class trial.   *"Hands up those who think 'C' is to blame."*
Just a few hands were raised and the same with 'B'. Most of the class condemned 'A'. Beyond severe disapproval and anger, 'A' was not punished. Because Mr Crofts was so liked, we were all miserable under the weight of his extreme disappointment in us. He totalled up the cost of a new pane of glass, plus a gallon of petrol for the return trip to Derby which was half a crown. In all a total of 25 shillings (£1.25). To meet this bill we were told to bring in contributions which were posted on a class list.

Even under the kind protection of my teacher, I was held in low esteem and was a favourite class target. To compensate for this persecution, I conceived a plan to appear more wealthy than the others. Owning a shop selling 'posh' items in a coal mining area gave this idea some impetus. Had my parents been more articulate, and more disposed to talk to me, wiser council would have warned that this strategy was doomed to failure and indeed later, did make matters worse.

Mum was persuaded to donate one whole shilling and I was thrilled to see the list publicly displayed on the classroom wall for all to see. My twelve pence made a stark contrast next to the ones and twos of the other boys.

After a frosty period, Mr Crofts once again warmed to us.

In my career as a teacher on both sides of the Atlantic, I have never experienced such an entertaining and stimulating classroom. His technical and practical skills, enterprising ingenuity has over a long career inspired thousands of pupils. Peter Crofts had not only imagination, but gave up a great deal of his free time working hard and incurring no small expense.

Mundy Street Boys School, January 1954.
Mr Crofts on the right with a slightly smaller class of 36 boys.
Top row standing from left to right - Colin Calladine, Donald Poundall, Roger Neal, Ronald Parkin, Bobby Fowkes, Kenneth Driver, Alan Parkes, Trevor Clarke, Roy Hufton, Michael Parkin and Jeffrey Barber.
Centre row standing - Keith Tinsley, Terry Brailsford, Robert Hardy, Graham Hibbert, Max Theobald, Michael Cope, John Elliott, George Bonsall, Michael Jackson, Mall Stirland, John Wilson and Tony Holmes.
Front row seated - John Thompson, Terry Hart, Andrew Latham, John Smith, David Gillott, Alan Buxton, Stewart Hutchinson, Eric Townsley, Chris Ward, Derek Knighton, David Needham, Alan Leatherland and Brian Mee.

In the summer of 1978, I was interviewed along with several other candidates for the position of History Teacher at a large comprehensive school. Many searching questions were asked by the headmaster who was by inclination traditional and strict with pupils as well as staff. He asked me to comment on discipline. The answer given sealed my appointment.

"Discipline is of paramount importance. Without good classroom management and control, there is no point trying to teach anything."

56

Many of us can remember struggling teachers who presided over a cacophony of chaos. I have seen them as teachers and colleagues. The skills which produce a respectful and orderly class owe a lot to the presence and personality of the teacher. Mr Crofts was a good classroom manager, and I am inclined to the view that he also achieved popularity which is even more difficult.

The Smalley Parish News of April 1997 reported - *"His pupils rarely misbehaved, hypnotised by his stare and unruffled pose - seemingly unperturbed by any situation"*. He is one of the foundation stones of my professional teacher training. He gave sound examples worthy of emulation. Quite different to the progressive left wing teacher trainers, lecturers and professors in Britain and the United States, who paraded their bankrupt child centred ideas some fifteen years later.

I was never formally punished by Mr Crofts, but on a few painful occasions, received the sharp edge of his tongue. That he should have been cross and disappointed was for me devastating. On this point, to the best of my memory, I think I speak for the majority of the other boys.

One unfortunate dirty scruffy deprived pupil frequently suffered the humiliation of others not willing to stand next to him in line. Amid jeers of *"stench"*, *"nits"* and *"the lurgy"*, my tormentors decided to push me next to him. To my shame, I resisted and was quite rightly publicly reprimanded for considering myself to be better than this poor individual who had never done me any harm. Mr Crofts was protecting this boy making it clear to the whole class that such conduct was unacceptable. In exactly the same way he protected me, as I discovered to my cost when he left for another job in the spring of 1956.

I was bewitched by his portable wind-up gramophone. Oh to have got my hands on it! It must have been old even then because he said -

"I wish it would break down so that I could buy a new one."

An enthusiast tells me that it was probably a HMV 202, manufactured between 1939 and 1946. Mr Crofts told us the story of the Student Prince and we heard the voice of Mario Lanza. Other beautiful pieces were Handel's Messiah, and on warm spring evenings I fondly recall "All in the April Evening". It was enjoyable to sing -"The Hag is Astride this Night for to Ride". He tried to introduce us to classical music and criticised "The Man from Laramie" as a popular song which would be forgotten in a few weeks. Sorry Mr Crofts, not my favourite, but 43 years on I can still remember it, having forgotten much of the "serious" music you played!

These were the days of some inane works in the 'hit parade' as it was called in those days. I was especially irritated by "Oh Mein Papa" and much worse, "Twenty Tiny Fingers". Like my teacher, music was to become very important to me, albeit our tastes were vastly different. As a pre-teen, I was thrilled at the ecstatic first taste of the type of popular music which was to become very "serious" indeed to my generation. This particular 'Golden Age of Music' is subjective and personal, but is roughly between 1957 and 1963. The exaltation of first hearing "Why Do Fools Fall in Love" was at the very conception of 'Pop' preceding the exciting sounds of Billy Fury, Adam Faith, integrated with the wonderful days to follow at William Howitt Secondary Modern School.

My fifteen months with Mr Crofts were definitely the best part of my four years at this Church of England School. He liked flowers in the room and urged us to bring them. Another chance to please my teacher! I eagerly arrived one day after lunch with a small bouquet, only to be met by a cool and angry Mr Crofts who had just inspected the inside of my desk and found it a mess! During his admonition on my untidy habits, he noticed the flowers and softened slightly to thank me for bringing a little colour to the class.

The first clearly remembered history lesson was here. He told his keen quiet respectful audience how the teenage Henry VIII was a multi-talented prince who deserved to be king. We enjoyed writing about, and drawing pictures of archery and jousting. I wonder if any of the lessons given by Mr Annable will be recalled as clearly and fondly in the year 2035?

The desks were probably originals from the first day in 1891. Old, good solid sturdy quality, but now worn, tired and ink stained from the days of our fathers and grandfathers. Nearly half a century from that time, I often think of those boys, many of whom will now be grandfathers themselves. Mundy Street School now spans four generations. In the first 64 years of its existence the writing technology of this Victorian school was still Victorian - wooden pens with metal nibs which were frequently dipped into the pot ink well. I remember
58

precious pieces of useless over used blotting paper and the teacher's supply of dark blue powder which was mixed with water to make ink. It took some skill to write neatly without making a blot! A sin which spoiled your work and attracted a sharp reprimand. A ball point pen was not expensive but not permitted. Here close to the Millennium, tapping away in front of my computer screen, I no longer have to worry about making a blot!

On one beautiful summer afternoon, Mr Crofts said - *"On such a day, I am not staying in!* Would that I could have done the same in the 1990's! Today a great deal of red tape is necessary to take a class outside the school premises. All parents must sign a form giving permission. On this day we were treated to a long and interesting walk along the Erewash Canal. Under the warm sun we studied sticklebacks and water boatmen. Another walk (or was it the same one) took us to explore the 13c. Codnor Castle. Little did I know that four decades later I would be floating over this ancient ruin in a hot air balloon. A pity I did not join the other holiday trips to Devon and Cornwall and the Norfolk Broads when we enjoyed the scandal of Alan Draycott falling into the river! At some point I was taken in a group by Mr Smith and Mrs Joyce Crofts to the Earls Court Motor Show. Possibly 1957.
Drama was represented by the unscripted "Toad of Toad Hall". Great fun being entertained by the ad-lib acting skills of Trevor Wilson.

Our accomplished and energetic class teacher once produced a carrier bag containing the raw materials of firework manufacture. I loved fireworks. To our gratification, a demonstration mixed with many cautions followed. The Smalley Parish News tells us - *"Once during a chemistry lesson, he accidentally set fire to his hair. Determined to maintain his calm and ignoring the shrieks of concern from his pupils, he taught on to the end of the lesson. The scar remained for many years!"* It reflects credit on Mr Smith that he was able to tolerate such a comprehensive and dangerous curriculum.

On safer ground we had a class election inspired by the General Election of May 1955. There were about five candidates including the teacher. He promised more modern schools with central heating and electric lighting as opposed to his rivals who spoke of longer holidays and free chocolate. Mr Crofts lost miserably achieving only four votes.

59

I can now reveal that he would have had one more - but I was coerced into supporting another. I think Keith Tinsley, a popular boy, won the election.

E.150 (P. & S.).

DERBYSHIRE EDUCATION COMMITTEE.

SCHOOL _Junior_ Dept. _____

REPORT for ~~Term~~ Year ending _22nd July_ 19 _65_

Name of Pupil _Narvel Annatte_ Age _9, 11_

Class _3_ No. in Class _32_ Average age of Class _10, 10_

Subject.	Marks	Out of.	Position
Arithmetic	20	101	32
English	64	130	24
Spelling	11	20	
Geography	7	30	
History	12	30	
Nature	8	30	
Music	2	20	
Scripture	1	20	
Handwork	15	20	
Art	15	20	
TOTAL	144	421	

Class Position - 29th

Times absent _1 out of 132_ Times late _0_

Conduct _Good._

Progress _Good._

REMARKS _When Narvel joined the class he had to learn to write like the others._ Class Teacher _P.R. Croft._
This held him back for many weeks. We have been very pleased with the way he has tried. Head Teacher _____

60

No one can accuse me of showing off with regard to my July 1955 school report! Nevertheless this unflattering set of miserable results is now useful in criticising modern reports. Little did I know that when Mr Crofts was painstakingly writing down these poor scores; one day in the distant future I would wield this same report as a stick to hit the progressives!

When I started teaching in the 1970's similar reports were still being written. Now at the end of the 1990's some are computer generated, as was the case in my comprehensive school where left wing management controlled what we could, and could *not* say. These modern reports do have advantages. They are professionally presented and it is possible to give a depth of verbal detail in an economical space of time.

Mr Crofts indicates that my conduct was good. Had I been a disruptive nuisance and bone idle the whole term - he would have stated just that. Some of my difficult pupils fell into the above category, but unlike the Mundy Street staff, I had a limited number of statements to choose from which were couched in positive terms. So the lazy boy who has spent the year raising hell, driving his teacher and other conscientious pupils mad, takes home a report which tells his parents -
"John sometimes distracts others, but we are confident his concentration and effort will improve next term."

I was not allowed to award marks on exercise books, or indeed to record them anywhere else. On the report itself there was no provision to indicate numerical marks, grades or class positions. No one was top or bottom, just a dull grey equality of tame comments. In many schools today, 'competition' is a dirty word. I was once 'carpeted' for telling a mother that her daughter had come 'top of the class'.

For each class I compiled positions and displayed a TOP TEN in the room. After the style of the 'Top of the Pops' the occasional announcements of the Top Ten became an exciting and enjoyable feature of the lesson. Fellow class mate wanted to know who had done well. They looked forward to seeing the new entries, and the ones who had been beaten by tough competition and dropped out. All were encouraged to do as well as they could. One day my Top Ten was spotted by the left wing deputy head. She took them down and I was given a reprimand in her office on the grounds that it was against 'school policy' and unfair to the other 20 pupils. Exit Top Ten!

61

If parents are alarmed at these changes, the solution is in your own hands. Complain! Attend parents evenings and insist that marks are recorded in exercise books. Require class positions on reports. Strongly suggest that desks are arranged in rows facing the teacher instead of noisy groups. Demand that teachers are addressed formally and respectfully by surnames. The progressives have only been able to make their damaging changes in the last four decades because we have stood by and let them get away with it.

In 1955 my parents had to face the harsh fact that I was weak and most of the other boys had done better. Coming 29th out of 32 said it all! At the foot of these gloomy results were the kind and mitigating comments of my teacher who gave me encouragement and the benefit of the doubt. This is the correct function of written comments. This 43 year old document gives precise and accurate information not present on today's modern 'progressive' reports. The worst result appears to be scripture (RE). Perhaps a reaction to the ethos of a Church of England school. One out of twenty is a stark reality, but in 1998 there would be no numbers only a euphemistic comment such as -
"Narvel has learned some of the basics of Scripture."
Reflecting the fact I scored at least one mark which is better than zero, but Mr and Mrs Annable would not be allowed to know this. Nor would they know that every single class member did better than me at Arithmetic. It would be - *"Narvel has mastered a few fundamentals and is making slow progress."*
Thank goodness for the invention of the calculator!

On my visit to Mr Crofts, I drew his attention to the neat and well formed writing from his dip nib, the same as used by the boys. His response was surprising, humble and touching. *"I was writing my own report when I wrote this one."* Apparently Mr Smith was very strict and fussy about the style of script he expected from his staff, and insisted that Peter Crofts re-learn to write in the fashion of Mundy Street. In the age of the word processor we have left these standards behind.

Around this time I proudly took delivery of my first bicycle, a red Raleigh, Triumph Palm Beach. Even in periods of straightened circumstances, my parents had always been generous financially. This single item must have cost them a little short of the average week's wage.

Dad patiently helped me to acquire the skills of cycling, launching me on the nearby quiet Abbott Street and the Recreation Ground. At the end of each hazardous and uncertain launch, I simply had to 'fall over' when arriving at a full stop, until the dismounting technique had been mastered. On my first 'long journey', all of two miles, I accompanied Mr Crofts who was cycling on the way back to his new marital home in Smalley. The trip had special significance for various reasons. It was the first occasion in which I had exclusive sole social access to my teacher. Previously I had been one of a few boys who, from time to time, would help him tidy up after school. It was an exciting experience for a lonely isolated withdrawn working class child. Here was an adult, a smooth sophisticated well educated middle class gentle man, talking to, and giving me his full attention as we progressed along the pleasant Heanor to Derby Road. Here also was the beginning of a life long love of cycling, my principal pastime giving me access to the beauties of Derbyshire. On arrival I was invited into the comfortable looking house, offered tea and made welcome by Mrs Joyce Crofts. I floated back to Heanor in a bubble of blissful joy savouring this privileged adventure.

Forty one years later, a recently retired teacher visited that same friendly home for the second time. Researching this book, it was necessary to arrange to interview the Crofts who were, I was delighted to discover, still in residence. The reception for the man had the same warm hospitality as that offered to the boy two generations earlier. Traces of the once fresh handsome face of the young man were still discernible in the gentleman who spoke to me in March 1996.

As we went down the memory lane of Mundy Street Boys School, I continued to address him as <u>Mr</u> Crofts. At no time did he ask me to call him Peter, even though I was now over my half century, had a university degree and a career of secondary history teaching behind me. When researching for William Howitt Secondary Modern School, it came as a surprise to find that, for the most part, staff did not know each others Christian names! They simply addressed each other as Mr, Mrs or Miss. Having finally located Miss Brentnall, the games mistress, I had difficulty pronouncing her new married name of 'Cirillo' Taking pity on my struggle, she kindly said - *"Just call me Freda"*.

Mundy Street Boys School, February 1955.

Mr Crofts is on the right of this large class of 46 boys where I make my first appearance.

Top row standing from left to right - Alvin Kerry, Jeffrey Ward, John Smith, Brian Mee, Robert Hardy, David Gillott, Keith Scarle, Joe Cauldwell, Terry Hart, John Thompson, Graham Parkin, Edward Wilson and Tony Benniston.

Centre row - Peter Brown, John Cauldwell, Allen Cookson, Eric Townsley, Victor Birks, John Wain, John Elliott, Tony Holmes, Tony Driver, Arthur Aldred, Alan Draycott, Allan Semper, Roy Hufton, Leslie Cope and Narvel Annable.

Front row seated - Malcolm Stirland, Leslie Watson, Keith Tinsley, Kenneth Musson, Tony Lowe, Ronald Parkin, Alan Buxton, Trevor Wilson, Desmond Atkins, Allan Carter, Michael Stoddard, David Pulford, Andrew Latham, John Kemp, Peter Watson, Alan Leatherland and Victor Beeby.

* * * * * * * * * * * *

Miss Beryl Briggs later told me -

> *"Freda was the youngest of the staff, and the only*
> *one who was always called by her first name."*

To us, of course, she was <u>Miss</u> Brentnall - no relation to the deputy headmaster, Mr Maurice Brentnall. In my experience as a teacher, the general unwritten rule was that staff addressed each other by their surnames within the hearing of pupils. It came as a surprise to find that my first authoritarian headmaster at the comprehensive school, actually <u>had</u> a Christian name when it was revealed in a leaving speech. It was always <u>Mr</u>. The succeeding jolly headteacher bounced on the stage and said - *"My name is Tom Jones, but please call me 'Tom'."*

Fortunately that was the only change with regard to names. We were spared the horror of Belper High School's example where I am given to understand that pupils address their teachers (even the headteacher) by their Christian names! I disapprove strongly of this practice which corrodes the sacredness of the pupil - master/mistress relationship, where some emotional distance is required to maintain the necessary authority and respect to do the job.

That was the first and last interview with Mr Crofts. That one hour in which I made valuable and copious notes was all the more precious, because shortly afterwards I heard that my venerable teacher was suffering from an advanced and terminal disease. As Mrs Crofts said later - *"You caught him only just in time"*.
He was unable to speak to me again. Almost to the week one year later, Peter Raymond Crofts died at the age of 67. His funeral on the 14th of March 1997, filled to capacity St John the Baptist Church, Smalley where he was the organist for 39 years.

Some weeks after the funeral, I searched out one of my old two and a half inch Ordnance Survey maps, and decided to find and re-visit Codnor Castle. A cool easterly wind tempered what otherwise would have been a warm sunny April morning, replete with raucous cawing crows and the song of blackbirds. Despite a dry spring, bright lime green had not failed the grass or healthy hawthorn.
This had been my first castle to which I had been drawn by thoughts of a revered schoolmaster. Craggy crumbling grotesque shapes could be seen in the outline of the southern wall which appeared strangely top heavy. Ancient windows, chimneys and dramatic zigzag cracks due to age or subsidence completed the picture. In the various graffiti, worn by decades of weather, I half expected to see "Peter loves Joyce" carved into the old stones. In her loss Mrs Crofts could take some comfort in the knowledge that she had shared her life with such a man. If I knew him so little and thought so much, just think of the impact he had on those nearer. I did not know the man well, so the tears must have been for a part of my life which was attached to his memory, rather than the man himself.
He was kind when kindness was in short supply. He made a big difference, touched my life, set an example, steered me to the profession recommended by Thomas More when he said - *"Be a good teacher"*.

65

Mundy Street Boys School, March 1956.

Mr Crofts on the left with this more manageable class of 26 boys.

Top row - Alan Semper, Alan Dunn, Peter Watson, Leslie Cope, John Kemp, Barry Brough and David Pulford. *Centre row* - Kenneth Robinson, John Cauldwell, Allan Draycott, Leslie Watson, Geoffrey Ward, John Wain, Kenneth Musson, John Smith, Arthur Aldred and Thomas Kenmuir. *Front row* - Brian Whitehead, Peter Brown, Ronald Rouse, Allan Cookson, Narvel Annable, Brian Capewell, Trevor Wilson, Tony Lowe and Martin Camm.

A Strict and Stern Headmaster

To my little eyes, Mr Smith the headmaster was the pinnacle of authority who had been there in absolute power forever. It would never have occurred to me that there were two headmasters before him, or that 55 years before my very existence, there was no building at all! As I looked at that ancient stern countenance, it was inconceivable that at one time back across many summers and winters, Leonard Smith was once a young boy like myself.

Mr Crofts had to share his classroom with the office of the headmaster and vice-versa. A small section near the door at the north end of the west wing, was delineated by bookcases as the inner sanctum of Mr Smith. His head would occasionally rise above the parapet, to the irritation of my teacher. *"Is that the second time you've had to speak to that boy Mr Crofts?"* At some point later we were delightfully distracted by hammering workmen who constructed the wooden walls of a new office on the same site for the headmaster. This small room is still there today. Privacy had arrived for teacher and headteacher alike. A battery-powered red light was affixed above his door. Clear and formidable instructions were given to the effect that if the light is on, Mr Smith is in conference and must <u>not</u> be disturbed. This particular pupil would not have dared go near that door irrespective of the condition of the light!

Mr Crofts observed that Mr Smith's level of noise tolerance was low even in a situation where a high level would be reasonable. In the playground he objected to unnecessary screaming and shouting. Here I will stake a claim to share a common attribute with Leonard Smith. One fondly remembered compliment once paid by a senior member of staff at my last comprehensive school which I would like to have on my tomb stone - *"He kept a quiet room"*. I do <u>not</u> subscribe to the modern theory that a noisy room is a place of learning.

In the Hall of Mundy Street Boys School during morning assembly, we stood in stillness and silence as Mr Smith raised his long tapering baton calling us to song. A baton is not a cane, yet I still saw it as an instrument of oppression. It was there and then that I acquired a life long detestation for the religious music called 'hymns'.

> *"To whom the lips of children*
> *Made sweet hosannas ring"*

One of his frequent favourites, this dismal doleful dirge vividly recalls my personal despair of the day. I am told this particular song of praise, exclusively for Palm Sunday, is meant to be bright and cheerful! For one unhappy little boy it will forever be associated with humiliation, pain and suffering. It must have been always Easter at Mundy Street, and was all tied up with the musty odour of compacted boys, stifling lack of ventilation and Mrs Wycherley on the piano. I looked longingly at the high open window, hoping some fresh air would come in and less likely, that I might fly out to freedom away from the pain of school, home and Heanor. In later years it came as a surprise that some people actually liked hymns! I thought they were deliberately composed to be depressing and dreary to enable the suffering singer to atone for his sins. The sacred song of Psalms were also sung on a dull, daily basis. A mechanical monotonous recitation - up and down / up and down. At one point we had to stand rigid, look straight ahead and chant the Apostles' Creed, the formal authoritative statement and affirmation of the Christian faith - "I believe...."

Mr Smith spoke his kindest words to me on our first meeting in December 1954 when my mother visited the school for the first and last time. He was concerned about my safety coming to school and was pleased that I needed to cross the road only once. Interesting to note that the danger was so keenly perceived at a time when car ownership was rare. After that I found the headmaster distant and fearsome. His authority was more subtle than the cane brandishing Mr Barlow of Long Row Big Boys School at Belper. The traditional teacher side of me greatly respects Mr Smith. Before addressing him, one had to say - "Please Sir....". Passing him - "Excuse me Sir".

Philip Justice attended Mundy Street School from 1960 to 1964 being one of the last batch not to take the 11+ exam and one of the first into the brand new Heanor Gate comprehensive school. Unlike the author he has affectionate memories of Mr Smith and the school. One point of strong agreement is on Mr Smith being one of the last effective guardians of courtesy, good manners and respect for elders. For some recent years Mr Justice was a reprographics engineer visiting local schools in the course of his duty. He was appalled at the "rude pushing and jostling" he endured trying to navigate the corridors. *"In my day, if a teacher or any adult visitor was approaching, we stood aside, **well** aside. You would not **dare** make physical contact with their sacred person."*

At my comprehensive school, I quickly learned that it was wise to stand back from the crush of moving pupils through a door. Some staff short of time braved the experience and received the same apportionment of shoving and jostling (and sometimes worse) suffered by any other person. The fact of being an adult and a teacher bestowed no privilege at all. It was better to wait and maintain one's dignity.

Mr Smith was also strict with his staff. He regularly checked that all exercise books had been properly and thoroughly marked. A teacher's spelling error would always be spotted and commented upon!

There was no shoving or jostling, but plenty of "Please Sir" and "Excuse me Sir" on the morning of July 6th 1998. The place, I am delighted to report, was Mundy Street Junior School when I re-visited after an absence of forty years. It is a joy to find that both my old Heanor schools are still run on traditional lines. The odds were against this. Mr Kelvin Gibbs the young headteacher showed me round his well organised school which appeared to be populated by extremely polite, busy, neat and happy boys and girls. In such a warm welcome, the old Dickensian hell hole seemed much smaller and had lost its bite. The hard edges of the playground had been softened with flower boxes and interesting colourful features. The cruel memories seemed very distant listening to an enthusiastic Mr Gibbs and his obviously very competent staff. But this modern confident headteacher was not the cheery progressive I criticise in other pages. This friendly headteacher (if it was needed at all) was prepared to 'name and shame' any offenders! A well structured policy of sanctions calls for the miscreant's name to be written on the blackboard if an initial verbal warning is ignored. Punishment is balanced by an equally well structured encouraging array of rewards and honours. Result - an excellent modern Mundy Street School!

My experience as a pupil and later as a teacher, has taught me that children are fascinated by the private person behind the facade of the professional who stands before them. As the teacher is more strict, so the interest is the greater. The cheery progressive who is happy to let the kids 'do their own thing' in a rowdy child-centred environment has much less mystery. The awe inspiring pedagogues of my generation, the likes of Miss Florence Calder, Mr Thomas Geoffrey Barlow, Mr Leonard Smith and Mrs Maud Buxcey held a high level of intrigue. They set out a barrier beyond which we could not cross. Mrs Smith said her husband could be friendly but was never familiar with pupils or indeed his staff. To function properly as an effective teacher, I had to disregard the advice of modern teacher trainers and modelled myself after the style of the likes of Leonard Smith. To give credit to his memory, I am deeply grateful for his example.

Mrs Winifred Molly Smith was kind enough to give me a glimpse of the private person of Leonard Smith. She was sad to hear of my woe and wretchedness under the stewardship of her late husband and said -

"If only you had told your headteacher!"

A child is imprisoned in its own private network of fear and dread due to peers and the adults who control and organise his life. Modern children are educated and encouraged to be aware of their rights, assert them, and ask for help - one welcome and positive aspect of the progressive movement. This was far from the case in the 1950's, and I remained locked in my own personal hell. The commonly received wisdom of the day said that boys should fend for themselves and deal with their own problems. *"Hit them back",* was the usual unhelpful response to a tentative timid complaint. You had to sink or swim. I sank. With the exception of Mr Crofts, for the most part, staff were indifferent. One particular teacher, on several occasions, actually encouraged my tormentors. Beware of the child you abuse. He may one day grow up and write a history book!

Ten years before, Barry Forster had spoke of - *"...the show of strength, so typical of a boys school, but an accepted way to form the pecking order. After school there were frequent fights on the rec', but woe betide any boy seen fighting by a member of staff!"*

I often heard the expression to 'have him out', and physical violence was an ever present threat at Mundy Street, but my problems were mainly psychological from taunting, derision, humiliation and social ostracism.

It is good to know that the old adage - *"Sticks and stones will break my bones, but names will never harm me"*, has now been thoroughly discredited. Ill treatment at Long Row Big Boys, Belper, was more physical, knock about, and bearable than the carefully crafted sadism of a few Mundy Street boys. Mrs Smith assured me that the headmaster would have interceded on my behalf had he been in full possession of the facts. *"He was always for the underdog, having been one himself."*

She described him as a 'small man', which came as a great surprise! The daunting and impressive Mr Smith had appeared to be a giant to the author who was after all, a boy at the time. This headteacher may have lacked height, but had not been short on stature. Armed with this interesting information, I studied one of the school photographs and noted that he was indeed only marginally taller than the row of standing boys. His wife went on to draw a contrast between Leonard the schoolboy and myself.

"Being small he was frequently picked on, but didn't bottle it up.
He was prepared to fight."

Mrs Smith, born in 1908, is a native of Swadlincote, ten miles south of Derby. Leonard Smith, was born in 1905 at the nearby village of Woodville. Another surprise was to come. He failed to pass the equivalent of the eleven plus and his mother paid the necessary fees for him to attend the Ashby-de-la-Zouch Boys Grammar School during the First World War. Here we begin to see a similarity between young Leonard and his future pupil some 40 years later. His academic ability may have been modest, but his effort and determination was great. Unsatisfied with his job as a clerical worker in the local colliery, he decided to fulfil his ambition to become a teacher. As with myself, burdened with a poor school record, this was against the odds and involved considerable difficulty. Notwithstanding, he pursued his chosen profession with resolution and tenacity. I am full of admiration for those who spend years attending night school. After a full day at work in which the employer has had the best from you during the optimum early hours, the evening sees one mentally tired and ready for a rest. Leonard Smith battled on to complete his Cambridge School Certificate and worked hard to achieve a degree from Leicester University by a correspondence course. His main subjects were French and History, but later studied German. At a time when foreign travel was not common, the Smiths went abroad every year and he was able to converse fluently in Germany and France where they had friends.

So after all Mr Smith did <u>not</u> spend his college days studying "All Glory Laud and Honour" and Mrs Smith did not recognise the 'Ayatollah' I described in an early paper on Mundy Street Boys School, but she did confirm that he was a devout Anglican and sound Christian which guided the principles of his life.

Over the years, at each visit to the hill top market town of Heanor, I see Mr Leonard Smith. The stark, dark stony image of the immovable massive 15th century tower of St Lawrence Church and the stern countenance of the remembered man - are one and the same. Similarities have been forged during a young vulnerable period through my harsh personal experience. Like the headmaster this ancient landmark (front cover) of the Erewash Valley, the outline of Church and Power, has survived change and stood the test of time.

In one assembly he made a disapproving reference to a football match being played on Christmas Day. Emphasising indignation to his congregation of quiet respectful boys standing at full attention, I can still see that raised tanned bony finger accentuating all key words.

"I am mad about football, but on the birthday of Our Lord,
my place is in church!"

A comment remembered 40 years later must have made an impression in my young head. I recall thinking - what an appalling choice of these two equally hated activities, on the <u>one</u> festive day of my otherwise miserable year!

These were the golden years for sound quality education and discipline. The above recollected incident exemplifies the fact that we were all listening with rapt attention. Standing in neat rows with a respectful rigid bearing, hands out of pockets, motionless mouths not mobile with gum, not fidgeting, not shuffling from one foot to the other, heads facing the leathery countenance of our Master, not daring to be distracted. How very different to the so called relaxed and enlightened assembly of today! These would have been the same high standards that Leonard the boy would have experienced. I am envious of Mr Smith the headmaster who was fortunate to have no progressives to challenge his tried and true philosophy.

The veneration of the headmaster of Mundy Street Boys School was carried through to the caretaker - Mrs Whittaker. Mentioned by Barry Forster, she was there in the early 1940's. A pleasant lady and always spoken of in the most respectful terms. Woe betide the boy who was rude to Mrs Whittaker! She worked very hard and it was not always pleasant especially when I recall the appalling state of the toilets whose walls were sometimes decorated with lines drawn by excreta! The courtesy shown to Mrs Whittaker puts me in mind of the underpaid, under-respected and much abused dinner ladies at my last comprehensive school. Out of the other members of staff they particularly liked me! This was because I would *not* pass by when it was clear that they were in difficulties with objectionable pupils. I helped. Long gone are the days with the likes of Mrs Whittaker.

The first appointment of Mr Leonard Smith as an ordinary teacher was at a school in Woodville. In 1943 at the age of 38 he became the head-master of Mundy Street Church of England Boys School, where he would be secure solid and all powerful for the next 27 years. Winston Churchill was once heard to say - *"If only I had the power of a headmaster!"*

At the same time as I escaped from Mundy Street Boys School, and descended down the hill to Loscoe Road School in September 1958; a certain Miss Mary Watson (later Mrs Holmes), left Loscoe Road Girls School and ascended up the hill with the first set of girls to help form the new Mundy Street Mixed Junior School. Both schools underwent major re-organisation into co-education, and the Loscoe Road School was re-born as William Howitt Secondary Modern School. Quite a change for Miss Watson who had been accustomed to total separation of male and female staff at Loscoe Road Girls School. She eventually became the deputy head and worked with Mr Leonard Smith until he retired. *"He was the fairest, kindest and one of the most understanding generous people I have ever met. Totally committed to his school, pupils and church before and after retirement. Very small physically, but professionally he was brilliant. He never had to raise his voice and never lost his temper with anyone. As soon as he walked into a room there was silence. Respect was shown straight away. He was a strict disciplinarian, but never had to resort to anything more than a short rebuke."*

Much of the above is consistent with my own recollection. The cane was never used at Mundy Street Boys School in my time - a complete contrast to Long Row Big Boys at Belper. However when pressed Miss Watson did agree reluctantly that Mr Leonard Smith -
"...did not generate warmth."
Some contributors unwilling to be named <u>did</u> share my memory of the little acetous and feared headmaster, who in spite of doing a good job, appeared to be aloof, cold, restrained, detached, haughty and forbidding. For even balance, it should be said that at my last comprehensive school, a number of pupils would have gladly applied the above description to the author! It is probable that the presence of Miss Watson, girls, and advancing years eventually mellowed Mr Leonard Smith.

When a former headmaster is welcomed back to the school by his successor, it is a fine tribute indeed! Mr Ian Ottewell took over the position in 1970 until he retired at Christmas 1993. Miss Watson tells us *"We had some wonderful assemblies and Mr Smith being a brilliant pianist was asked back to play for the morning hymns."*
At the age of 60, Mr Smith was suffering from a heart condition and retirement was recommended, but this conscientious educator was happy and contented in his valuable work. He persuaded his doctor to - as he put it - *"...keep me going"*. He was able to give a further five years of good service to the children and parents of Heanor, up to the traditional retirement age of 65. This puts me in mind of my first teacher, Miss Florence Calder, the formidable and greatly respected mistress who taught for half a century at the long since demolished Bridge House School at Belper. She reluctantly retired at the age of 76 in 1953 and is the subject of my first book "Miss Calder's Children" - A Social History of Belper, Biography and Critique on Modern Education. Contrast these two examples with the current stampede to escape from stressful teaching at the very earliest opportunity - in my own case - age of 50! Premature retirement has increased 50% in the last ten years and now four out of five teachers get out before the age of 60. (The Daily Telegraph - 9.1.97.) Had we not given in to the

progressives and allowed our children to get out of control, the above sad statistics would not be telling their grim story.

It is an extraordinary coincidence that in 1979 Mr Leonard Smith collapsed right outside the very school to which he had devoted his life. He was going to the Heanor Citizens Advice Bureau where he was a generous and reliable helper. He died shortly afterwards. Having enjoyed only nine years of retirement, he had reached the age of 74.

In contrast to my own personal recollection, he is generally remembered with affection. Mrs Smith tells me that on many occasions she has been stopped in the street by ex-pupils and parents who have enthusiastically expressed gratitude for the care and professionalism over the years from her much respected late husband. He was greatly valued and sadly missed.

The Eleven Plus Examination

It would have been in June 1956 that I sat my eleven plus examination in the Dickensian hall of Mundy Street Boys School. The invigilator was Mr Hubert Chambers the headmaster of Loscoe Road Boys School. He had some occasion to ask my name, but before I had time to answer, it was delivered by a boy on the next desk. This was irksome as it made me look stupid - which was no doubt the purpose! I had not a hope in hell of 'passing' this all day exam. To the best of my memory it consisted of mathematical problems, an intelligence test in the morning, and English Language in the afternoon.

The committee of Sir Henry Hadow in 1926 had accepted the wisdom of psychologists that the inherited ability of a child could be accurately measured. After struggling in vain with the various puzzles, conundrums and shapes that morning, I am delighted to report to the reader that the 'Intelligence Quotient' - IQ, has now been discredited. One of the few occasions in which I can cheer with the progressives!

'Passing' the eleven plus examination simply meant that you had scored enough marks to obtain one of the limited places in the local grammar school. Depending on the places available, and the numbers of pupils, the 'pass mark' varied from year to year. For example the Heanor Grammar School may have had a maximum intake of three classes, each of 30 pupils = 90 places. The total supply of pupils from not only Heanor, but many village junior schools in the area, may be 900 pupils taking the exam and going into secondary establishments. Assume an even spread of marks, and it can be easily seen that the author would have needed to better a result of 90% to enter the hallowed halls of the prestigious Heanor Grammar School! In other words the eleven plus examination is no longer popular because it 'creamed off' the academically most gifted.

When Pam Carter was successful in entering the Heanor Grammar School in September 1949, she was in competition with children from Codnor, Eastwood, Horsley Woodhouse, Langley Mill, Loscoe,

Pinxton, Marlpool, Morley, Shipley and Smalley. Her own estimate put the elite group at something between 60 and 90 scholars which would have been a very small top percentage. Across the nation, on average it varied between a generous 40%, down to a tiny 6%!

"With limited spaces, great pressure was put on you to pass. All successes were printed in the Ripley & Heanor News and your mum would be stopped in the street to talk about it." In general terms the parental pressure was strong, but Mrs Carter made it clear that in her particular case there was a wider social obligation. An inferred coercion from teachers, Sunday School, family and friends.

*"In the small Heanor mining community of those days, when there was more structure to society; you were subject to a mesh of social pressure, including unspoken unwritten rules - which you broke at your peril! There was a perceived way to behave, and if you did something wrong, everybody was going to **know** about it and **talk** about you!"*

A pity these Heanorian rules were not explained
to me before I started Mundy Street Boys School!

Mrs Carter recalls the honour of wearing the blazer and school colours. Proud parents would hang up the school uniform in the front room window for all to see. Heanor folk had little money and often had difficulty paying for a coat, but a place in the grammar school had to be earned by merit alone and could not be bought by any amount of money. Heanor Grammar School started its life in 1894 when the old 18th century Heanor Hall became Heanor Technical School with Mr Ralph Stoddard as the first headmaster. These were the days when you could buy your way in, and Pam Carter's far seeing great grandfather paid for his five daughters and three sons to attend. Her father is also an old boy of the Heanor Grammar School which, together with William Howitt Secondary Modern School, finally died in 1964 with the birth of the Heanor Gate Comprehensive School.

Several contributors have spoken of a rivalry between the Heanor Grammar School and the 'Red and Green's'. This was the nickname for the Stainsby Hall private fee paying school at Smalley, attended by the sons of local professional and trades people who passed for the upper class of Heanor! Some remember these boys 'looking down their noses' at the sons and daughters of coal miners in the Heanor Grammar School.

78

Miss Mary McLening happened to be the invigilator at the 1949 11+ examination of Mrs Carter in which she was launched into -
*"A wonderful education, appreciated and valued all my life. But as one of the lucky ones, I am mindful that some see the system as unfair and things could have been very different had I **failed** to make the grade."*

I was interested to hear that the Grammar School was co-educational in all subjects except for games, woodwork, cookery and segregation in the playground. Young Pam enjoyed domestic science and looked forward to a regular visit from the Cosy Cat. This particular popular pussy, who must have seen more films that any of us; was a resident of the nearby (1922) Cosy cinema in the Market Place. Having no other home, it would wonder around the seats in the darkness and eventually find a friendly lap in which to settle itself. There was always food and good company at the Heanor Grammar School, where the girls would feed, fuss and cuddle the Cosy Cat.

Mrs Carter agrees with the comments expressed by my former teacher Keith Matthewman in Chapter 13 regarding co-education. She points out - *"The big world outside of school consists of men and women, therefore you should be taught to mix with the opposite sex. Anyway, I always liked boys! It was an essential part of my education. If it got to Wednesday, and you were <u>not</u> fixed up with the boy you were going to the pictures with on the Saturday - you started to get worried! Fond as we were, the Cosy Cat was just <u>not</u> the same!"*

The cinema was an important part of Heanor after school social life. She went on to tell me that when the lights went up; more important than the film, was to see who was sitting with which boy! The projector would often break down, and Pam remembers the unfurling of a large roll in front of the screen with printed words. In pantomime style, this was for community singing - *"..to stop the audience rioting!"* After repairs had been completed, the show went on.

Before her grammar school days, Pam Carter attended Lockton Avenue Girls School (1945 to 1949) which consisted of four classrooms in a raised wooden shed like construction, complete with veranda. Mrs Margaret Wright has happy memories of this small school which was located at the bottom of Beech Walk. Miss Crumpton the headmistress, requisitioned the Cosy cinema to show the girls a Sabu film. Young Pam remembers being taken to see a private showing of Pinocchio, organised to celebrate the birthday of 'Garth', Miss Crumpton's pet dog! In the Loscoe Road Girls School log book on May 19th 1919, the headmistress Miss Westland very neatly writes about one of her teachers:

"Miss Crumpton accompanied a class of girls to the swimming baths at Langley. This will be done each Monday afternoon at 3.00."

Nine years later on September 28th 1928 -

"Miss Crumpton left this school to commence as headmistress at the new Lockton Avenue temporary Junior Girls School."

Miss Lomax and Mrs Meakin were the other teachers in this little school which has long since disappeared.

Janet Hart (nee Shepherd) was one of the first girls to go to Mundy Street School when it became mixed, and soon took her eleven plus examination. She became a member of the fortunate few to achieve high scores, and was offered a place at the venerable Heanor Grammar School, but told her parents -

"I don't want to be dressed as a bee!"

This was a reference to the school uniform of yellow and black. Janet who described herself as a rebellious girl at the time, horrified Mr Leonard Smith with her determination to attend Aldercar Secondary Modern School. In his office, he remonstrated with her in the form of grave warnings of dire consequences coming from turning down a 'once in a lifetime' golden opportunity!

"For the rest of your days girl, you'll regret this foolish decision!"

Janet, a young girl, was under great pressure from the formidable headmaster inside his inner sanctum. She stood her ground, taking the view that her confidence would better hold up against less clever competition. Events proved her resolution correct.

"At Aldercar Secondary Modern School I always came top of the class, and could now tell Mr Smith that he was wrong."

After the initial pride had worn off, young Pam had similar views on the glaring yellow and black -

"I looked like a demented wasp! To try and tone it down, I wiped my blazer round the cloakroom floor."

According to Mr RA Butler, the original purpose of the proposed eleven plus in 1944, was to place young people in a secondary school which took account of their 'different interests and abilities'. RJ Cootes tells us *"The 'eleven plus' examination was to decide whether children should go to a grammar or technical school, with an academic curriculum, or to a modern school, where the emphasis was on practical subjects. This system of selection was soon widely criticised. Many doubted the wisdom of making decisions about a child's future at such an early age, especially as the exam itself was not always reliable. Newspapers in the 1950's carried stories of 'eleven plus failures' obtaining university degrees."*

Thanks to the Campaign for Real Education, I took part in a debate on Central Television's programme called 'The Jury' on the 14th of July 1996. My job was to condemn the wanton destruction of our excellent grammar schools, and praise the traditional practices which maintained the high standards associated with selection. As one who had never been a pupil at a grammar school, I could not be accused of being a beneficiary of the 'unfair system' as it was called by the opposing team of progressives. In this I felt qualified, competent, but uneasy, arguing the case against the typical comprehensive school. I tried (and failed) to make the point that perhaps a compromise could be achieved with setting, or banding, inside a single campus. This was the case for the first few years in my last comprehensive school under a traditional headmaster.

When the camera had stopped rolling, one of my more vociferous opponents angrily turned on me as a 'traitor' to the cause! He was irritated and could not understand why I supported a divisive system which had demonstratively failed by my personal example.

Having never seen the inside of a grammar school, I did perhaps have an exaggerated reverence and respect for these prestigious institutions. A reverence and respect which irritated some of my left wing lecturers at Matlock College, who were only too keen to destroy these centres of excellence. I was deeply impressed with the high standards of Matlock Grammar School during my 1977 teaching practice. Masters entering the classroom were received in silence by upstanding neat respectful quiet boys. It was a dream! The finest teaching experience I have ever had on either side of the Atlantic.

These idealised perceptions of the Heanor Grammar School with its hallowed halls and dreaming spires, were called into question by information from an ex-pupil John March who was there in 1958. He remembers it being more rough and ready with pupils <u>not</u> always rising on the entry of staff. *"On the contrary, some teachers were locked **out** of their rooms! I have a vivid memory of a master who had to climb through the window! We flirted ink stained blotting paper up to the ceiling. It would stick up there until it dried, and then fall down - great fun! We rebelled against the uniform by bending the rules such as wearing white or coloured socks. Into the 1960's some of the girls tried to get away with short skirts. Caps were supposed to be worn, but this was not always enforced.*
I was happy at the Heanor Grammar School, but it failed to teach me study skills which would be needed for university."

Interesting views were expressed on the BBC Timewatch programme called 'Grammar School Boys' 14.4.98. The ex-Chancellor of the Exchequer, Kenneth Clarke, who very nearly attended the Heanor Grammar School said - *"The eleven plus exam suited me down to the ground. It was designed for the likes of me. A working class lad from humble origins who had a chance to compete with the privileged."*
Barry Hines the author took a different view -
"Going to the secondary modern meant you'd get a labouring job such as being a brickie, or a joiner, or go down the pit. Grammar School meant an office job with collar and tie to sign on, rather than clock on."
Neil Kinnock criticised the system because -
"It was an appalling cruelty. The failures were cast into the outer darkness and were never expected to succeed ever again."

As you will see in the second half of this book, the happy and successful pupils of William Howitt Secondary Modern School had <u>no</u> sense of failure or being 'cast into the outer darkness'. The 'Camelot' of Queen Mary McLening was a winning place in every sense of the word - even for those in the class of Mrs Cook!

Bullying

When Mr Crofts left Mundy Street at Easter 1956, it was a loss to the school, but an even more serious loss for me. The protector had gone and I was delivered into the hands of my enemies! The event is marked by a memory of a disabled drivelling boy called Johnson. I was intrigued by the compassion and consideration from the other boys when he would join us from time to time usually for outdoor events in good weather. On Sports Day a few pupils staged a mock race in which the struggling cripple was allowed to win with rapturous applause. His mother smiled at the scene thinking what wonderful good natured boys they were. Little did she know. I envied his twisted body with leg irons, wondering if such an affliction could bring to me a few kind words. The 'rough and tumble' of Heanor youth had its own code of ethics and in this I was considered 'fair game'. Although they never saw me cry, the local word of 'mardy' was occasionally used to describe my loathing and unwillingness to take part in any kind of sport.

Bullied children today have the advantage of knowing that such conduct is totally unacceptable and incidents are widely reported and analysed in the media. To his credit my last headteacher at the comprehensive school was prepared to move heaven and earth to root out a bully. It was the only activity which seemed to spur the progressive to punish with speed and efficiency.

Researching this book, people have been amazed at the clarity of my memories. Good, equally as well as terrible incidents stick firmly in the mind for all time. If childhood recollections are lost to the majority of those looking back, perhaps it is because their days were less eventful, less ecstatic and less agonising. Retrospective ability does vary. To my surprise, one boy in my class, has almost no memory of Mundy Street Boys School.

On a few rare occasions my situation would deteriorate to the point when I could not find the courage to go to school. A new brown mock leather jacket had been acquired and was promptly, and no doubt jealously, phlegmed on. Using paper towels, in the plain utilitarian cloak room, I cleaned off the disgusting thick mucus, but without mercy, this upsetting incident was repeated later. It was on the very same afternoon that one boy, in front of a small amused audience, was making unpleasant comments about my mother. Deeply humiliated with outrage, I muttered some reference to his own mum, but he only had to threaten to force me to withdraw the comment. Shamed and debased, the next day I pleaded with my unwilling parents to support me in the lie that I was too ill to attend school. They   took the view that the 'slings and arrows' of the outrageous cruel world had to be faced and dealt with, but under pressure, being lenient, reluctantly agreed.   Father went off to put in long hours, driving his old rickety ramshackle green bus. It was used to ferry the Lovatt opencast workers to and from the outcrop at nearby Codnor. Mother went to attend her little shop of ever decreasing profits. I was home alone savouring a relative calm and respite, until I heard ominous footsteps along the narrow dark entry between Buckberry's tobacconist shop and Michael Reed's. This was the ultra modern bright young men's outfitters, beloved of the Teddy Boy generation, some few years my senior. Loud knocks sounded at the door, which fortunately had a small aspirin sized peep hole. Cautiously and quietly, I descended the entrance stairs and peered through to find an alarmingly familiar face, excited bobbing around, keen for an answer. A boy in my class had been sent by the class teacher to investigate. Stealthily I withdrew and waited in hope that the unwelcome visitor would give up and go back to the evil hell from whence he came. To my utter horror he tried the door, found it unlocked, entered and ascended up to the first floor and main living area of the flat. I had managed to creep up and hide in a small box cupboard at the head of the second flight of stairs leading to the bedrooms. Faintly I heard the young intruder taking his sweet time to investigate the main front living room, kitchen and then the bathroom. Holding on to the hope that he would eventually get bored and leave, I remained very still. Matters could hardly get worse - but they did. He climbed to the second floor bedrooms. Having not quite closed the box room door, the snooper curiously gave it a little push. The resistance to a full opening was not my person behind the door, but the clutter around me. He considered the partial view of the junk filled interior for

84

a moment, but an eternity for the cringing pathetic child only inches away. The reader may be angry thinking -

"Why didn't you challenge this rude brazen trespasser,
who surely would already be in deep trouble?"

Perhaps the answer has something to do with power and the inexperienced victim behaving like a victim. Only three years on, the self-assured adolescent, the confident confidant of Horace Hart would never be in such a situation - but this, alas was the reality of 1957.

Satisfied, and much to my relief, he prowled on to the principal front bedroom of my parents to which I will refer later. A brief look as it was rather neat and presumably uninteresting. His prize discovery was the second bedroom upon which was attached to the door a child-like crayoned sign which incorrectly spelled out - 'PRIVET'. Mortified I heard the click of entry to my own inner sanctum. The agony of this moment was not based on any fears of burglarious activity. To the best of my knowledge, the inmates of Mundy Street were totally honest. No, this individual was after a more sadistic objective - to bring low one who had already suffered much, and in this, as we shall see later, he had a powerful friend. Leisurely he set to examine all parts of the interior which included the contents of drawers, diagrams and pictures on the walls, clothes, books, comics, toys and all manner of personal effects. All this took quite a span of time for a miserable child now cold and huddled nearby. Descending steps announced the end of the ordeal. The measured unhurried creaks seem to enhance the cruel satisfaction of the exercise and the smug hint of smile could be imagined. The door closed - he had gone.

Arrival at school the next day confirmed my worse fears. Seeing my stony expression and sensing blood, a gloating and smirking group gave me to understand that the scout had delivered his report to the master, publicly in front of the class after the style of a jocular account which was received with noisy rapture and merriment. Included in this 'entertainment' was a reference to the 'Privet' sign, drawings on the wall of the ubiquitous space rocket, a painting of an American car, comics considered too young and other useful targets. This event is unbelievable by modern standards of the belated war on classroom bullies.

If the boy who explored my home (now a man of 53 years) is reading these words - I would like to say this to you. You are forgiven, but I find it more difficult to forgive the adult professional hand which sent you and (if it was true) allowed you to humiliate me in front of the whole class.

One notable occasion was so awful it actually stilled the taunting tongues. Maths cards of varying degrees of difficulty were given out. In obedient silence we laboured, but one boy went to the front, approached the teacher who was quietly poring over some document.

"Please sir, I can't do these. Can I have another card?"

Quite rightly he was corrected to 'May I' and the request granted. Emboldened by this example, a second pupil approached the position of power and successfully returned with an easier card. It should be pointed out in fairness to this teacher that serious staff shortages had caused the merging of two classes - about 80 youngsters in one room, under the responsibility and control of one man. The lot of a master in normal conditions, of an already over size class of 40 frisky lads, will produce considerable professional stresses and strains which the author knows to his cost! But here the author was a boy who could not do his sums and had seen two examples of how matters may be helped. Very slowly and reluctantly, after the mood and style of Oliver Twist, I approached this man who had never shown me a scrap of kindness and courteously asked for more simple sums. What followed stunned both myself and all the other boys. He turned his angular pale bony face to me, lifted his hand and struck me hard across the face three times. The modern word of 'gobsmacked' would seem to be the most appropriate for that staggering moment. The shocked and dazed class stared at the standing numbed victim, possibly waiting in vain for tears - of which there were none. I have no memory of a change of card, nor of a return to my seat.

Perhaps it was this arithmetic incident which gave me to suspect his conduct with regard to an English Composition. We were told to write a story. A task I enjoyed as it exercised my imagination. In spite of weak writing, spelling and grammar, here was a chance to demonstrate some small ability. Like a repeatedly abused dog, I **still** wanted to make a favourable impression on my master. For a full lesson I took pains to produce a neat script, not blotting my paper, creating a loud colourful character called Captain Hic Hadared. His

86

ship and crew were caught in a storm and whirlpool, dragging them down to a deep and improbable cave-like air trap. In short a strange new world. A likely inspiration from the combined works of Jules Verne and Robert Louis Stevenson, but I was satisfied and considered it original. The next day came with an unpleasant surprise when we were all harangued for sloppy pathetic attempts. Our English books were piled on his desk, at this time back to the usual class of 40. To correctly mark 40 short exercises would have been a conscientious feat. He said they were **all** bad and claimed that he could put his hand in the pile and pull out any single one which would demonstrate the appalling standard of English. His hand went to the centre of this pile. I was not alarmed. My chances from 40 of being selected were remote - and in any case, my effort, so I believed, was reasonable. A moment later in mock sneering tones he was reading the story of an unfortunate captain and his sailing ship descending into a spiralling whirlpool. Like his fictitious captain, the unfortunate author endured more uproarious laughter, catcalls and ridicule, but unlike Hic Hadared - there was no safe place to hide. Rather like the official legal wording of a medieval torture : *"...as much as you can bare - and greater."*
Forty one years on, and in view of other incidents not all told in these pages, I cannot believe that pure chance brought out my work on that day.

It was a further, similar degradation during the hated games which brought me to the point of considering a drastic and permanent solution to my problems. Worse than pointless to ask the class teacher to intercede, and much too fearful to approach Mr Smith; I begged and pleaded with my mother to telephone the headmaster, as I knew she would not go to the school in person. After putting up the usual objections (ignore them, hit them back etc.) she agreed to my proposed simple quick easy option of ringing up the school. Accordingly a message was sent to the class teacher to the effect that Mr Smith wanted to see Narvel Annable. In those days it was not the custom for a child to enjoy any measure of privacy, and no one was surprised when the teacher aggressively demanded to know "**WHY?**" before allowing me to depart. Obediently with a terrified weak voice, I trembled out something connected with being pushed in the mud and a telephone call to Mr Smith. This was followed by barracking and catcalls from the assembled multitude. Furious, and astonishingly, he said that I was getting him into trouble! Stupefied, silent and rigid, I waited for the order of dismissal. The short journey to the classroom of the teaching head was on the outside of the building. We were not permitted to go through the hall or other classes in session. This was an appalling walk I shall never forget. Halfway there and away from all eyes, for the first time I broke down and sobbed without restraint. The persecutors never saw tears at Mundy Street Boys School. Perhaps I was still under the influence of the formidable Miss Florence Calder who said once to Bess West - *"Keep your tears in your pillow."* A few minutes on and now composed, a clearly harrowed boy was briefly interviewed by the headteacher. Not much changed except a new resolve of my own.

Children in my position desperately unhappy at school and home usually run away to join the gypsies, the fair, or perhaps go to sea. But since Heanor is a long way from the coast and no gypsies were about - my thoughts turned to suicide! Having considered this drastic solution my despair was suddenly lifted. I felt better. There was a way out. This darkest period occurred in 1957 when we moved to No 4 Red Lion Square above C.S. Buckberry the confectioner and tobacconist. The builder's date is still there - 1888. 69 years later on a dull wet afternoon a miserable tormented boy was looking out of the second floor bedroom window into the drizzle, all the way down the long distance to the bottom of High Street. Then down to the glistening pavement below and wondered if the drop would be great enough to kill quickly. I am so glad I did not jump! It would *not* have been sufficiently high and I would have ended up like the Johnson boy, deprived of all the happiness to come at William Howitt Secondary Modern School the following year.

This culture of cruelty was interrupted by one significant incident. A boy in our class called John Wain had passed his 11+ and achieved a place in the Heanor Grammar School. Before the age of the comprehensive school, we the unsuccessful looked at this mysterious academy for the chosen few with awe. John was telling me that apart from difficult homework from time to time, his new school was OK. An unremarkable conversation. The significance was his friendliness, courtesy and charm; qualities from a fellow pupil to which I was unaccustomed. Thank you John. I will always remember that brief and civilised exchange 41 years ago. I wonder where you are today?

88

The American Dream

As this, the darkest year, progressed, there was one particular hope which is best called 'the American Dream'. In 1952 my younger sister had met a GI and emigrated to the United States. Letters from America were exciting and promised a better future for my working class family. She once telephoned and in those days the cost was £5.00 for a three minute pre-booked trans-Atlantic call - which was equivalent to about half the average working man's weekly wage. With ears glued to the phone I remember the local Derby operator with the Derbyshire closed 'u' and absents of 'h's, talking down the line to the London operator. He in turn with cockney tone spoke to the nasal New York girl who communicated with the drawling young man in a noisy clacking room somewhere downtown in hot humid Detroit. Eventually the Detroit voice said "Go ahead Derby" and little humble Heanor was (possibly for the first time ever?) connected to the Motor City at a 4,000 mile distance. Thrilled by the technical wizardry of our voices passing along an under ocean cable, Mum, Dad and self were enthralled to listen to a close family member with her sparkling chromium plated American accent during a rather inane and yet emotional conversation.

Unlike Belper, the Langley Mill exchange was not automatic. Each telephone was accompanied by a little black box with a handle which had to be vigorously turned to ring the operator one mile down the hill. Telephones were not common in this little pit town. 'Mrs' in the flat below would never touch the device no matter how long it would ring! She was fascinated by our 12" Ferguson television and very nervous at the roar of the Hoover vacuum cleaner.

In the 'Land of the Free and the Brave' all these things were common place, only bigger and better. The American Dream became an obsession as I thoughtfully sat below the hissing gas mantle of Mundy Street Boys School. I milked the trans-Atlantic theme for all it was worth. All things American were wonderful. One day I would go to Detroit and live happily ever afterwards! A fellow pupil, Brian Mee had gone to Australia and proved that escape was possible. I wonder if like me, he also returned? I once waved a picture of the New York skyline in front of Mr Crofts. *"In't it good!!"* I forget his response. The 'promised land' did eventually become a reality for me. Disembarkation took place from the old Queen Elizabeth one day before the assassination of President Kennedy and within weeks I became a confirmed Anglophile. The old old story! Happiness is not in the future in another place. Happiness is here and now. The knack is to find it, but nobody told me that back in 1957.

Eight years on at about 3.00am on a cold January night I was nearly falling asleep leaning on my stout yard brush on a third floor gantry, the air thick with the pungent gasses and dust of molten metal: thinking of the green Derbyshire hills and clean English air. But my half closed tired eyes could only see a dismal dark desolate sight of industrial blight, tangled black ugly metal of the vast unending Great Lakes Steel Mills, Wyandotte, Michigan. Another five hours to go before I could clean up and get to my bed at an ungodly and unnatural hour. This was the reality for my 'American Dream' and was one of six different jobs before I finally went to college. But it was all experience and 1965 was, if not the happiest, certainly the most eventful year of my life and the subject of my third book - "Cycling Out in 65". Watch this space!

Back in Heanor, one day I was 'unwillingly creeping' back to school when an extraordinary event occurred. Walking up the right side of Market Street a little way up from our shop - I stopped dead in my tracks and stared. It was beautiful, stunning and magnificent. A visual orgasm symbolising all the promise and hope of the future. It was everything to love and I loved every part of it as I slowly walked round this long low wonderful orgy of dazzling chrome. My eyes caressed the knife blade fins, with their rocket launcher taillights, and were delighted by the aggressive bullet bumpers. It oozed power and seduction, occupied a wide swath of the road, but common-sense and practicality was put on hold when this dream machine was conceived. Motionless it was, yet one knew that in motion it would glide in silence and complete superiority. I gazed through the tinted huge wraparound glass windshield onto the bright array and multiplicity of controls. Automatic transmission, air conditioning, power antenna, power steering, photoelectric beam adjuster and of course - cruise control. Do
90

not forget reader that we are still in 1957! Forty one summers and winters back. I would have given almost anything to possess this beautiful American car. At that moment on Market Street in Heanor on that day, I found all the other cars small, ugly, dull and contemptible.

Suddenly my ecstasy was interrupted by the realisation that I was supposed to be on my way to school, now late and in grave danger of receiving the wrath of the teacher.

The morning of Friday, December 6th 1957 is particularly painful to recall. Headline news reported that the Americans had made a failed attempt to launch the first United States artificial earth satellite. Later newsreel footage showed the Vanguard Rocket crumpling back to the ground amid an inferno of exploding flames at Cape Canaveral after achieving barely ten foot. The tiny 14 kilogram sphere in the top cone was still pathetically sending out its radio 'bleeps' when the stricken vessel lay prostrate. The classroom teacher made comment on this exciting latest news. He reminded us that only two months before to the day, the Soviet Union had astonished the world by, for the first time ever, putting into orbit an artificial 'moon' six times heavier. He added further weight to the Russian cause by drawing attention to the event of November 3rd, when the Communists had launched a device thirty times heavier in which a dog called Laika was testing conditions for the first manned flight. The thrust of this lesson was to show that the Americans were well behind in the space race and the other boys took full advantage as they leered over, jeered and enjoyed my discomfort and humiliation to the full. At one point he said "The Americans are afraid of the Russians" which caused some to mock machine gun me. This ordeal was tolerated and eventually ran its full course. A popular American song of the day by Perry Como ran - *"Catch a falling star and put in your pocket, save it for a rainy day."* This was sung at me in the playground, but with altered words - *"Catch a falling satellite and put it in a match box, send it to the USA."*

More pain was to follow. By February 1958 there were a total of five failures out of seven attempts to launch a satellite from Florida. All Russian rockets were successful. After all, we would hardly be told of failure!

Forty years on, Barry Brough, a pupil in that group spoke of his main memory of me. Interestingly it was not a recollection of a

91

tortured miserable child, but of a weird boy who was always in a dream world about rockets and space travel. At every opportunity in class, I took pains designing and drawing sleek fantastic alien missiles. In the playground I could be seen walking round and holding a horizontal pencil which represented a futuristic vehicle many light years away from the troubles of Mundy Street.

Barry recalls other lads saying - *'Is ay a bit funny?*
At which Barry would reply - *"Nar, ays rate, it's just in 'is 'ead!"*
Apparently amidst hooting derision I had said a man would one day land on the moon. A prediction of which I have no clear memory, but Barry graciously pointed out that events twelve years later had proved me correct. The supply of small cigarette size picture cards of stars and planets inside Brook Bond tea packets gave me a small hold and measure of protection from Geoffrey Ward who was a collector. Barry was the first ex-pupil of Mundy Street Boys School approached, on the grounds that I had no unpleasant associations with him personally.

"I should think not", he said with a measure of indignity.
"Me and Noddy used to stick up for you!"
'Noddy' was Martin Camm, Barry's *'best pal'* who he described as *'small and frail'* and also in need of guardianship. As I was <u>not</u> little and weak, perhaps the others saw me as 'fair game'.

But life was not all school. My bicycle had given me a new found freedom and once in a while I followed the open road west in search of kindly Grandma and Granddad in far off Horsley Woodhouse - all of three miles from Red Lion Square! The simplicity of my working class family was only slightly changed by a brief encounter with the relatively sophisticated Jewish business world during the war. Although buying and selling had brought us a measure of prosperity, events were proving that my parents had not the skills, luck or aptitude to survive in retailing. Give them credit they <u>did</u> take the risk, make the attempt and soldiered on for over ten years.

But it was in 'Osly Woodas' that I saw the true nature of my coal mining heritage. 'Oop tag 'ill' and down the other side and up again, and the Derby Road had delivered you into the open countryside for which I have much affection. Red Lion Square (back cover) is at the foot of Tag Hill which has the reputation of being the rougher part of Heanor, and a travelled reputation which is interesting and colourful.

Derek Goostrey tells me he has heard people talk about it in Blackpool! The name originates from the necessity of having an extra horse 'tagged' on to the team. This was to help haul heavy loads up the steep gradient in the days of the 18c Derby-Mansfield turnpike. A turnpike was a cruel looking gate guarding a privately owned road. To use it, you paid a toll to the keeper at the gate or bar. This was fortified by long vertical spikes or pikes to dissuade you from avoiding payment by forcing your horse to take a jump! Hence the name turnpike.

From our living room at Red Lion Square, showing the one third of a mile straight view towards Loscoe Road School.

The date of '1888' is to the right of our front living room with Connie Annable at the front window. Above - the 'window of despair'.

My grandparents were typical gentle ordinary people. Commonly and roughly spoken, but actual swearing was taboo in the Annable clan. I am given to understand that my dad Samuel (1913-1972) the youngest son, was the only one of the six children to utter an occasional forbidden word. This strict moral code was partly down to the influence of the old building on my left (south side) as I cycled through the village centre.

It is said - *"Annables! Oh yes, they're chapel folk"*.

Granddad, Joyce and Grandma
with Nell the dog.

The Horsley Woodhouse Central Methodist Church celebrated its bicentenary in 1997 and has strong connections with my family. The Heanor Howitt lads of the late 1950's, who thought that the Horsley Woodhouse lads were a bit rough and wild, might be interested in a comment written by a Dr Gregory in 1840 -

> *"The boys of Horsley Woodhouse are the most*
> *aggressive little ragamuffins I ever saw!"*

I am grateful to Freda Staley for the above, and also organising an interesting display (25.7.98) of memorabilia, old photographs and documents, which included a fascinating project of the history of Horsley Woodhouse written by Steven Millhouse when he was at school. We learn that our family village was mentioned in 1225 with regard to one - Thomas de Wudehus.

'Wudehus' - isn't that the way we have always said it!

Together with many other names, there are six 'Annable' bricks on the front, each indicating a donation to the original Sunday School room which was added to the chapel in 1904. You can still see the large inscribed handsome wall clock which was presented in 1905 by my great grandfather - Isaiah Annable, born in 1843!

With a name like that, who could be older?

His parents were older. Thomas and Ellen Annable were born in 1817 in the reign of George III, the king who went mad. On my left at the north eastern end of the village, I had cycled past 'The Croft' a

94

substantial detached property some 50 yards north of the main A609, which was the family home of Isaiah Annable and his wife Mary Annable nee Eley. It was then known as 'Bardills Lodge' and accommodated their eight sons and two daughters. The third son, Fred (1874-1971) married Sara Jane and sired a boy called Willis one hundred years ago in 1898. When he was 16 he became a student teacher at the Smalley Richardson Endowed School. It was to be a short career - two years. He resisted the call of the ubiquitous pointing Lord Kitchener to fight for King and Country and do battle with the Hun. Conscription was introduced in January 1916 and Willis was a single and fit young man whose name started with 'A'. The letter which also stands for Abbeville, a town in northern France situated on the River Somme. 'The Somme' will always be associated with mud, blood, pain, death and destruction on a massive scale. The young teacher was still a teenager when he was gassed and blinded in 1917. He was taken to the British hospital at Abbeville where he died three days later.

The fourth son, Arthur Annable, eventually built a house called 'Ash Leigh' (number 214) which is on the north side of the road taking name and shelter from the large tree opposite, now sadly axed like far too many trees before their time. Arthur Annable and Hannah Hebb had three sons and three daughters, all now long dead. Even today that part of the village is relatively quiet, and four decades back it was very peaceful after busy Heanor. After the 'clink' of the ornate front gate, I will always remember the same surprised greeting at the side kitchen door -   *"Well - well - well - well!!"*
Time seemed to have stood still in that musty old Victorian home. The shallow stone sink still had a large fluted cast iron disused hand pump over the well, and all rooms showed evidence of gas lighting. The old rooms seem to hold the gentle love of the long time occupants, a wonderful contrast to me after the cruel classroom to which eventually I would have to return. A variety of nostalgic smells are affectionately recalled, the most pleasant was the pipe of Granddad in the middle living room. A great ancient man deeply settled in a shapeless comfortable easy chair amid a haze of blue smoke. A well earned rest following a lifetime labouring in the bowels of the earth. After a smile of greeting, he had very little to say to me. The women in the kitchen,

Grandma and maiden Aunty Joyce were more loquacious. As Arthur was born in 1879-1960 and Hannah in 1878-1964 respectively, my grandparents were in fact 78 and 79 in 1957, not an impressive age by the standards of today.

But the memory serves up a primeval trio. Grandmother's face under her grizzled hair was deeply etched in leathery wrinkles rather like the apples she occasionally gave me. Of course Joyce, 1919-1985, was only 38, but she was old in every other sense. Never seen with make-up, dressed in dowdy old fashioned style, she absorbed the influences and old thinking of her parents, spoke and moved slowly with a slight stoop. She was not stupid but her mind had never been challenged having such limited experience of people, travel and the wider world. In their cosy kind contented narrow habitat, I was for a time - safe.

I was usually offered, *"...a bit o' balm bread."* Delicious with the hot tea from a bygone brown teapot. The primitive kitchen table was hard up against the wall to which they sat, facing the old sash window, but at right angles to the normal position. Eating and drinking was always carried out through a seemingly uncomfortable 90 degrees. Years of unnatural contortion had trained the spine to accept this unhealthy posture. After a short time of small talk... *"Arrs ya dad? Arrs ya mam?"...,* conversation became more inane and less frequent until long slightly embarrassing pauses caused a small amount of tension. Into these silences Grandma would stare out through the window and ease the tension with a slow and easy - *...mmmmm.* A moment later Joyce made the same sound whose function was not clear, probably an affirmation of the previous inanity! Suddenly the bright clean surprise tinkle of a bell. To the rescue came - Joey. He was the pet budgie whose home was a bird cage which stood in the centre of the table. Not hygienic, but then a twelve year old in 1957 would hardly have noticed. At this point of dried up conversation, Joey provided a delightful distraction! All eyes turned upon the little bird. Our feathered friend cocked his head on one side and pecked his bell a second time. Grandma: *"Elo Joey."* Joyce: *"Elo Joey."* He responded with a single 'chirp'. Grandma: *Joey, Joey, Joey!* Joyce: *Joey, Joey, Joey!!* We were rewarded with another 'chirp', and he put his little head under the bell giving the amusing appearance of wearing a hat.

Grandma: *"Put ya 'at on Joey!* A chuckle from Joyce: *"Look Narvel, Joey's got 'is 'at on!"* Grandma: *Joey, Joey, Joey* .... and so on.

The trivia continued until my restiveness became apparent, and I made a restrained suggestion to the effect that it was getting late and I really must.... Then came (to my acquisitive young nature) the best part of the visit. Grandma would descend into the mysterious depths of the larder. Only several steps, but it seemed like an unending dark cave. She emerged generously holding in her thin bony old fingers - silver! Usually two half crowns (25p) and to my eager little eyes - a small fortune. *"Yo'll save this, wunt ya?"* I never did. Fireworks was my passion and every penny I had went up in fire, cracks, bangs, smoke and glorious Technicolor - each November 5th, next to Christmas, the most important day of the year. Poor Hannah Annable would have been horrified had she known.

Arthur Mee tells us about a connection between Bonfire Night and humble Heanor. *"A local lad Henry Garnett, born in the middle of the 16th century, grew up to be a central figure in the Gunpowder Plot in 1605."* This was the famous failed attempt of a Catholic group to blow up King James I and his Parliament. Ironically Garnett was the son of a Protestant schoolmaster from an unnamed school in Heanor.

"He fled to Hindlip Hall, in Worcestershire, where he hid four days in a secret chamber, nourished by broth and warm drinks conveyed by a reed through a hole in the chimney. At last he was driven out by foul air, apprehended, and finally drawn on a hurdle from the Tower of London to St Paul's Churchyard and executed."

I will spare you the grisly details and return to the cosy comfortable world of Grandma's house.

On my birthday they were also bountiful. The card from Horsley Woodhouse always contained a crisp old style large green one pound note and a crisp orange ten shilling note. The latter from Aunty Joyce. Thirty shillings in that day was a princely unstinting gift, evidence of their kindness and generosity. On the return home Mum would hear all about my adventures. Her hostile response to the trifling incident of 'Joey's hat' was surprising. The gentle and (as far as I could see) innocent Annables were bitterly denounced for their drab, pathetic and meaningless existence! *"Miserable old crows!*

Nothing else to do all day, but talk to the bird!"

97

Years later I discovered that after Connie Clifton (1911-1995) had changed her name to Annable, circumstances forced her to live for a period with the new in-laws - often a recipe for long term bitterness and resentment. This, on top of a cultural clash from the go-ahead adventurous personality of the girl from Stanley Common and the more slow, laid back, cautious, old fashioned Annable clan. Although from the same social station, mother was a glamorous woman, often seen heavily made up, laden with glittering costume jewellery, frequent and carefully crafted coiffure - always going out. Her wardrobe, many ensembles and impossibly high stiletto heels, gave her a 'film star' look of which I was proud. Your average Heanor mother, she was not. Despising the little drab mining town with its parochial inhabitants, Connie Annable considered herself wider reaching and more cosmopolitan. She made weekly visits to our Jewish friends in Nottingham and occasional business buying trips to London. In her more stimulating world, there was no time for the likes of Joey!

At some point Mrs, at 33 Market Street, in the flat below kindly suggested that the sad child in the flat above would benefit from a holiday and generously included me into her family for the precious annual trip to Blackpool for the years of 1955 and 1956. I was told that 'Mester' (Mr Boon) had written off to the boarding house to book the extra place. It was probably on the famous Albert Road, with its 'Saturday to Saturday, straight out after breakfast, ten in a bed,' reputation. In fact I had my own bed, but shared a room with her son Ken. We all seemed to move together as one body - Ken, Mester and Mrs, her sister Mrs Flinders and her son Arthur. A certain photograph, now thankfully lost in time, shows two laughing common looking women on Blackpool beach, standing in about six inches of sea water with dresses held up to knee level. In front a grinning skinny pale boy sporting bathing suit, hails the camera with a cheap air ring. A quintessential working class scenario - but what fun!

A more frequent method of escape from the pain of Mundy Street was the weekly visit to the Empire Cinema, just over the road. The magical beam, from the projection box took us all into another world on each Saturday afternoon. After standing in the raucous disorderly queue, we paid our three pennies and were seated row by row starting from the back.

Pam Carter remembers the 'Threepenny Rush' - *"All these rough kids were queuing round the corner into Fletcher Street. Because of the shoving and pushing, only so many were allowed in at a time by a huge man in uniform with epaulettes. He'd say 'That's enough!' - and fling out his big fat arm causing the whole row of scruffy screaming urchins to fall like a row of dominoes!*

At the Belper Palace it was seven pence but you sat where you liked - and I liked the front row. At the Empire, I was envious of one poor family, who for some reason were exempted and went straight to my first choice of seat to see an even larger Flash Gordon and bigger more menacing Emperor Ming the Merciless. The latter actually being my favourite, because I longed to have my own laboratory such as his. It was thrilling to see him moving from sparkling, flickering display panel to another, manipulating his many switches, knobs, levers, pressing buttons causing ever increasing cracks, bangs, exciting flashes and brilliant arcs of climbing electrical power. Seeing my own self in villainous black cloak and high spiked collar, I cackled and gave the tremulous order to aim the death ray at Mundy Street Boys School, after the style of Charles Middleton - the original Ming!

Kenneth Clarke, the ex-Chancellor of the Exchequer, told me that when he attended Langley Mill Boys School, he took a different view of Ming the Merciless - *"As a small boy, Heanor was the large town at the top of the nearby hill. It was worth the climb on Saturday morning, because 'SUPERMAN' was showing at the Cosy! It was so popular that you couldn't always get in. Down at Langley Mill we had to make do with Flash Gordon."*

A Fresh Start and New Life

My last report from Mundy Street is missing. Is it lost or did I destroy it? In July 1958, now aged 13, there was no reason for me to think that life would improve. We were all going to Aldercar Secondary Modern School, where according to my class mates I would be tormented even more and regularly beaten up by tougher bigger youths. The new showers were also threatening. Changing for PE or games had always been in the classroom and none of us had ever stood naked before each other. I dreaded this particular vulnerability and humiliation on top of the stories that the boys and girls showered together! Research has revealed that this fiction may have had a basis in fact. The showering areas of male and female were separated by a thin panel into which randy lads made peepholes! Janet Shepherd, the future Mrs Horace Hart, tells me that she spoiled the fun by blocking up their salacious view with tissue paper. None of this would have given me much comfort. Aldercar was an oppressive thought, but Miss Beryl Briggs who was the Senior Mistress from the birth of the new secondary modern in September 1955, assured me that my fears were groundless.

"It was not nearly so rough as my last school at Nottingham."

At some point I learned that my destination was going to be Loscoe Road School. News which I received with a cautious welcome. The day arrived. Not being quite sure where the site was located, I approached the newly born William Howitt Secondary Modern School from the foot of Wellington Road. All was confusion, hundreds of pupils aimlessly drifting around the campus. Groups of girls keeping themselves separate from the boys. Only one face was familiar from Mundy Street Boys School. Somewhere in that crowd were Derek and Barry Goostrey and Horace Hart, but these were unknowns at that time. Attention turned to the teachers. Standing on the veranda, they seemed as lost as the meandering hordes scattered before them. Suddenly! Ecstatic recognition! It was dear Mr Crofts!!

Only the formality of boy / master relationship prevented me from running up and giving him an affectionate hug. I was thrilled beyond

101

belief and asked if I might be in his class. He greeted me in his usual friendly manner and said that he had no idea as the situation was new to us all. Perhaps this was the auspicious sign that the tide has finally changed, the big change like the 'sea change' of Ariel's song from The Tempest

"Nothing of him that doth fade,
But doth suffer a sea-change,
Into something rich and strange."

The change was as much to do with adolescents as new circumstances. Hardly noticing, I was transformed from boy to man in the previous months. Even if my confidence and self esteem was still low combined with an apprehensive spirit, a deeper voice, taller stature and anonymity was to give me the advantage of a fresh start.

Eventually our names were called and we were organised into classes. Not the class of Mr Crofts, but it was immediately apparent that this new teacher had a gentleness and smooth sophistication, integral with his mature distinguished good looks. In addition he had a relaxed supreme confident class control which comes from years of teaching the tried and tested, free from the pernicious poison of progressive interference. This teacher had been at the Loscoe Road Boys School since at least 1927, 31 years earlier and is today as then, greatly respected and much loved by thousands of Heanorians. This excellent schoolmaster, now the Deputy Head of William Howitt Secondary Modern School had the proud name of Mr Maurice Brentnall.

We were in the most southerly classroom of the old girls section nearest to Holmes Street. Some of us knew each other and others did not. The atmosphere was uncertain and I was unable to tell how matters would develop. One clear early memory. We had an art / painting lesson. One of the few occasions in those days when desks are pushed together to form a group where pupils face each other. Around me sat big intimidating boys and I was watchful saying little or nothing. These were definitely the 'king pins' of the school, clearly older so I suspect the company included Terry Hutchinson, Pete Lambert and Terry Grace. They were busy and had prepared several colours. I needed a colour, blue in fact, so I reached over to get some powder for the job. One of the group noticed this, seemed surprised, and spoke. *"Use this youth!"* 'Youth' was a reasonably friendly address and the whole tone was surprisingly conciliatory. At the previous school, I would not have dared to assume permission sharing the property of another. A blue face might have been the result! An encouraging incident. I was now getting really hopeful.

This class was only a stopgap. We were tested to assess ability for streaming. These were the days when it was thought wise to place pupils in classes of similar ability such as a top, medium and bottom group. From a lifetime of teaching, I have found the modern method of mixed ability to be a disaster. In my last GCSE History class (1995) I faced an ability spread which ranged form near 'A' Level to a few pupils who could hardly read and write. All in the name of equality! It was impossible for me to aim a lesson at such a disparate group. The top were neglected and unstretched. The bottom were confused and lost - if they cared enough. Both extremes can and do become disruptive. In the early days of my last comprehensive school, (1978) sensibly we had an 'A' and 'B' band. If the latter worked hard, behaved themselves and came up to standard, they would be promoted into the top band. Lazy disruptive 'A' banders were demoted.

All this came to an end in 1986 with the arrival of a new progressive head<u>teacher.</u> A likeable friendly approachable man who has since appointed progressive senior managers who have, in education terms 'thrown out the baby with the bath water'. An example of this policy was to change the Special Needs Department which originally had small friendly classes taught by specialists who did an excellent job. At the time of retirement in 1995, these same pupils were taught by me - <u>not</u> doing a good job. In a class of over 30, I had neither the skills or time to deal with young people who needed constant attention.

Mr Maurice Brentnall tested us in English and Maths, the basic subjects considered to be indicative of general ability. The modern progressive would be horrified at the way results were revealed and announced. *"Hands up those who have full marks."* Just a few were visible, but the number increased as we descended and approached the middle scores of 5/6 or 10/11 depending on the size of the particular test. It was the lower scores in arithmetic which concerned the author.

"Hands up those with 3? 2? 1?" A few hesitant reluctant hands slowly went up to half mast in these lower regions. His eyes, kind and gentle as they were, came to rest upon 'yours truly'. Typical of this easy placid gentleman, and in an avuncular benign manner, he said. *"How many did you get Narvel?"* Hoping to become invisible and inaudible to all but the Master, I mumbled something like - *"I didn't get any Sir!" "Oh dear"* was the response. This ordeal was mitigated by a level of civility from teacher and pupils to which I was unaccustomed.

To the extent that I have no wish to embarrass weak pupils, I have come to think like the left wingers at my last comprehensive school. But at the same time, I would not rob the talented top end of their moment of glory by discouraging testing, banning all marks (below year 10) and published positions as I made clear in Chapter 5.
After about a week, marks were totalled in what must have been about three or possibly more classes of pupils ranging from 13 to 15. We were separated into three ability levels which for clarity I will refer to as 'A', 'B' and 'C'.

Names were called and a relatively small group of us were standing on the veranda. Little did I know, but this was to be the beginning of a wonderful rich experience as a small old lady approached us across the playground. Her most distinctive feature was the profuse and luxuriant cumulus white fluffy hair. On her large nose, which out of respect was never once referred to, rested blue fierce looking hawk styled spectacles, typical of the current fashion for ladies. These menacing glasses were at complete variance with the warm and kind wearer. 'Old' - she looked to us adolescents, but in fact Mrs Doris Cook was only 56 and as I later discovered from faded photographs, had never been attractive, even as a young girl. This cordial and benign teacher was beautiful on the inside - where it mattered. Her very first mild words were encouraging and propitious - something to the effect that we should follow her. Even her 'hen like' gait is well remembered, a bobbing deliberate tread as she led us to a wooden, light, airy classroom preponderant with glass. When we had sat down I felt a surge of deep satisfaction and auspicious goodness. Everything seemed right. Just out of the window was a healthy light green shrubbery and not far further were grassy areas and handsome mature trees. All in complete contrast to the darker hard viewless deadly interior of a
104

Mundy Street classroom. The Victorians took the view that windows were distracting and only the sky should be visible. Mrs Cook's post war class room was permeated with the happiness accrued from her previous presence in that place. I do not remember her words of greeting, but I remember well the feeling sitting behind the well kept lift-lid desks in that room in that September of 1958. It is a funny thing, you only cry when the pain has come to an end, and that night - I did cry.

As the morning moved on, I gradually became aware of the people around me. Good people, the nicest I had met since my very young days at Bridge House School, Belper. Here was a clue to the connection. The clement and considerate chemistry had a lot to do with the mixing of sexes. Girls and women are a civilising influence on the raw macho effect of an all male school. Boys tend to behave better in all respects under the watchful eyes of the more gentle sex. This last statement hardly fits the formidable Miss Florence Calder, but hers was a rule of kindness at the co-educational little school under Belper South Mill. It was as an eight year old that I first experienced the culture shock of Mr Thomas Geoffrey Barlow's Big Boys school, just over the road at Long Row. His cane swinging Ramboesque team, crashed in on my erstwhile cosy little life! Even here, and at Mundy Street, the hard masculine regime temporarily softened when the occasional lady was drafted in to ease a staff shortage. Girls seem to be more sensible, more mature, have a calming effect in shaming and reducing the yob element. So it was in the class of Mrs Doris Cook.

Sadly there was never a class photograph, but to the best of my memory, these were the pupils -
Geoffrey Abbott, Narvel Annable, Malcolm Caulton, Billy Havercroft, Barry Gillott, David Martin, Terry Miles, Jeffrey Ratcliffe, John Saxton, John Smith and Terry Sullivan. 11 boys.

June Benniston, Angela Brown, Jessie Fisher, Sheila Holmes, Brenda McKay, Carol Oakes, Pearl Shaw, Sandra Stainsby, Christine Thorpe, sisters Irene and Sylvia Walker.
11 girls. Class total - 22.
Lessons commenced which were pleasantly straight forward and simple, all from the same teacher. It soon became clear that this was a class

we would call today 'Special Needs'. Just as well, considering that I definitely 'needed' a kind patient teacher, 'needed' more cordial sympathetic class mates, 'needed' a more compassionate senior management and 'needed' the confidence and improvement of self esteem. Under the guidance and care of this excellent professional lady, I blossomed.

At my last comprehensive school, our hearts would sink when we were affronted by the sight of yellow slips in our pigeon holes, often dubbed 'yellow perils'. This meant that due to staff illness, we would have to teach a strange class for an hour, instead of having a precious preparation period. These few non-teaching interludes, used for marking and preparation, took the pressure off evening and weekend work at home. For me, the stern traditional who expected a quiet obedient group, it was particularly galling to deal with a frisky mob, sitting in groups, more used to the cheery progressive approach. It often meant an unpleasant hostile start, boys and girls lined up separately to be seated in rows on a random boy/girl basis. Left wing managers put me under great pressure to arrange the desks/tables in my own room in order that pupils could sit in groups facing each other - not the teacher. My instincts were to the contrary, having found that it encouraged idle chatter and constant distraction. These ugly beginnings to a substitute class were usually followed by a quiet lesson in which some pupils had to admit they were able to produce good work in a peaceful environment. Pupils of absent staff had no idea who would walk through the door to supervise. The greeting of a collective audible groan and pained expressions bore witness to my lack of popularity and reputation.

One rare cover I never minded was in the Special Needs department, as it was before the progressive policy had scattered them around the school in main stream mixed ability classes. You were always greeted with an amiable attentiveness by a welcoming little group which reminded me of the convivial quality in the class of Mrs Doris Cook. Credit due to the conscientious teachers who were hardly ever away.

In the years at my comprehensive school, this genial department had first been called 'Slow Learners' and then 'Remedial' before 'Special Needs'. Name changing seemed to be an attempt to alter the reality. Everybody at William Howitt Secondary Modern School knew the meaning of being in 'Mrs Cook's class'. It meant you were academically at the bottom and not very clever, but nobody in the other classes ever used that against us. Indeed if there was any 'shame' - it came from within as we will now see.

Author and Artist
Narvel Annable and Malcolm Caulton

Some few weeks into the term, Mrs Cook came into our pleasant room escorting a shy broody young man, who was further irritated by the introduction -
"This is our new boy, Malcolm!" followed by -
"That's a nice suit Malcolm." After a ripple of titters, he made sure we never saw that 'little green suit' again. A vacant seat at my side foreshadowed the start of a happy mischievous friendship. He sullenly sat down. Our first words are lost in the mists of time, but having taken stock of those around, he began to resent being put into such a lowly group. The lowest class in a secondary modern school could indeed be described as 'the lowest of the low'!

In fairness Malcolm's ability was well above the average, but his frustration soon found expression in 'mickey taking'. To my great delight he had a wonderful skill at cartoon drawing and I deeply regret the loss of these naughty efforts into Mrs Cook's waste bin! However they still exist in my mind. The raw material was perfect. We were an odd collection indeed, as is often the case in a low ability group. Malcolm's pencil spared very few. When Mrs Cook was angry, which was at least everyday, she had the habit of removing her glasses and saying *"Just a minute!!"* before the delivery of a sharp reprimand. A

107

hilarious caricature of this bit of business, depicting the piles of white hair, large nose and hawk glasses was produced which had me in hysterics. It was <u>so</u> good that I was certain she would enjoy a viewing and laugh with us. Declaring my intention of going to the front and grabbing the satirical sketch, the alarmed artist quickly snatched it back and said - *"NO! **God** no! She'd be furious. It's, - well it's - **insolence!**"* He had to explain to me the meaning of 'insolence' as my disappointment and laughter gradually subsided. Many times I have had to write the word in numerous incident reports over the span of my career. Malcolm would also have had to explain why his parody took precedence over the work we were supposed to be doing.

Other lampoons were less dangerous and poor Jessie came in for a lot of stick from us both. The teasing at some point turned to tenderness, as I remember at least one rainy date. It was the custom in those days to acknowledge an affair and produce embarrassment by calling the boy by the girl's name. Oddly I did not mind being called 'Jessie'. For me of little experience, and <u>no</u> success in that field, it was a triumph to have this liaison publicly known. Of course it would have been much more prestigious to be called 'Sheila'. She was the class beauty, well developed, much lusted after, but completely out of reach for the 'rag tag' likes of ourselves. Even though the boys and girls were much the same age, the latter seemed older and more adult. The attractive Sheila had the pick of mature teenagers and was already 'going steady'. She never looked down on us, was always friendly and pleasant but totally unsuitable for one of the cartoons.

Carol Oakes intrigued me with her charm, graciousness and air of dignity. So much so that we dubbed her 'Lady Oakes', she seemed to accept this title with engaging good humour.

Always laughing, I may have been, but at this point I was not actually the class clown. That honour went to Jeffrey Ratcliffe who was known as 'Sos'. This came from the boys at Smalley School who some years before had called him 'Sausage' due to his small stature. He had the reputation of being a character from Horsley Woodhouse. They referred to his dad as the 'stick man', who delivered kindling to the villagers necessary for starting a coal fire. Sos was often in trouble in class for one reason or another and the transgression followed by

"Come Out!" from an angry Mrs Cook. He seemed to wear a half grin / half ashamed look standing there at the front in his short trousers, uncomfortably shuffling around next to the annoyed mistress. Annoyed? Certainly in the first instance, but the riotous audience reaction, on more than one occasion, had her cracking up at the absurdity of the situation. When she moved he had the habit of jerking his head back in the expectation of a slap - evidence of previous experience. She never hit any of us. Sos had the quick skill of disarming her anger with a 'one liner' to take the attention off himself. Changing the subject completely he once pointed and said -

"Mish, that girl keeps lookin' at me!"

Poor Carol Oakes went deep red, nearly died with embarrassment as the rest of us were rolling in the aisles. Mrs Cook said - *"If she is, it's only because you've a funny face."* By this time none of us could remember what it was Sos had done to be called out in the first place.

On a more serious occasion, Sos had been discovered with photographs of **naked women**. *"COME OUT!!"* Once again the familiar short slow walk to the front as we desperately craned our necks and strained our eyes on the grubby little booklet in Sos's naughty little fingers. Beyond a quick flash of boobs, nothing could be discerned. Pornography in the late 1950's was very soft core indeed and very tame. Bare breasts were shocking by the standards of the day, but all genitalia would have been well hidden. These arguments would have been lost on the outraged schoolmarm as she ceremonially tore up the lewd obscene images into small pieces which drifted to the floor. Eleven pairs of lascivious eyes sadly watched the slow descent. A short lecture followed on the subject of filling our minds with wholesome thoughts and activities.

These were the days when our minds were often on sex, and yet at the same time on the perceived probability of sudden nuclear annihilation from a Russian atom bomb. The prospect of dying a virgin was a constant worry. These elements came together in a roguish inverted exchange with my classmate –

Narvel - *"Who, in all the world, would you **least** like to have a homosexual experience with?"*

Malcolm (looking serious, giving this great thought - after a few moments) - *"Mr Khrushchev."*

I was delighted with this excellent choice of the (to our young eyes) repulsive ruler of the ever threatening ominous Soviet Union. A vision of the little old bald rotundity chasing Malcolm around the classroom filled me with the giggles. *"Yield to Nikita capitalist boy, and let me remove zi leetle green suit."*

At further risk (Mrs Cook being near) and wasting more time, I continued this nonsense with a supplementary question -
Narvel - *"Who, in all the world, would you **least** like to have a heterosexual experience with?"*
Malcolm gave this question even more careful consideration. As the seconds passed, I eagerly anticipated a hilarious choice, and mentally willed him to name our strict diminutive box shaped history ma'am - 'Mrs Buxcey'. Eventually his face lit up and the result was well balanced and apt - ***"Mrs Khrushchev!"***

Disrespectful lads enjoying a slanderous puerile romp could hardly be expected to spare the unfortunate, but plump dowdy and grey, First Lady of Communism. Two years later, she was often cruelly compared to her beautiful and glamorous opposite number, Jacqueline Kennedy

Tug o' War on Sports Day *At the front - Peter Lambert, David (Rocky) Martin, Geoffrey Wilton, 'Ricca' Ratcliffe, ? John Lavender.*

A tiny but very significant courtesy is fondly recalled involving an animated class discussion. It lasted barely a second, but it will always be remembered and deeply appreciated. Terry Sullivan at the tender age of 14 was not only a good all round sportsman, but also a gentleman. Several of us were keen to make our points on some stirring subject when Terry and I spoke at the same time. We both stopped, made eye contact, he smiled and gave way to me with a nod. Mundy Street Boys School was just up the hill, not far away from recent experience. Such a polite kindness from a lad of some standing, a friend of David Martin, was totally unknown to me. Thanks Terry.

David (Rocky) Martin was the strong tough lad of the class enjoying the respect and fear which usually went with these attributes. But the vibrant up-beat personality was as big as the muscles. Always cheerful, everybody liked David, who never abused his power and was ever popular. He was a leading athletic celebrity and hero in my 'house' of Dale (yellow). Rated as one of the 'kingpins' of the school, he treated his subjects with respect and for this was all the more loved. Even so, Malcolm did not push his luck when inspired to draw the 'incident of the medicine ball'.

On one of the many hot sunny days of 1959 we had a PE lesson in the playground, and were suddenly confronted with wild threatening roaring Rocky Martin, glistening with sinewy sweat. Atlas like, he was supporting one of big heavy balls, and took it into his head to charge us with every intention of hurling the massive missile at our comparatively puny frames. Needless to say we shifted quick. This was the only time when our beefy classmate unnecessarily reinforced his top position.

A more gentle and chivalrous opportunity offered itself during one lunch time when Sheila Holmes fainted in the playground. It was the powerful David who cleared a path through the multitude, gently with no effort, picked up the limp maiden, and took her to the safety and quiet of Mrs Cook's classroom.

Mrs Mitchell took us for music. Like most music teachers of the day, she had little time or interest in our beloved popular singles in the charts, but on one occasion she did indulge David Martin. We were surprised but also elated when David's 'Hoots Mon' by Lord Rockingham's XI, filled the hall with its exciting, punchy, up beat bagpipe effect. After a bright and gyrating two minutes, a disappointing empty silence followed. Handing back the disc, she thanked David, adding a condescending comment to the effect that it was rather simplistic, repetitive and perhaps not the sort of music we should admire. A comment which irritated me.

Summer Cycling

During that wonderful summer, on many days after school, instead of going home, I cycled seven miles to the Herbert Strutt Baths in Gibfield Lane, Belper. It was an honour indeed when David suggested coming along! I will not claim a close friendship with this precursor to Horace Hart, but when brawny David associated himself as a cycling companion, with all the kudos which went with it - I was 'over the moon'! Little Sos came with us to add to the fun. Having been crushed by the dark years before, it is difficult to put into words the ecstasy from the mix of that adolescent scruffy trio, joyfully pedalling up High Street issuing shrieks of delight under the warm afternoon sunshine.

After the swim and an ice-cream, the three friends push biked back through Belper, up 'Bedlam Hill', eastwards to Kilburn where there was a separation. Sos lived at Horsley Woodhouse and David at Smalley, so they went up the hill towards Four Lane Ends. The previous Christmas we had 'flitted' to the village of my birth - Stanley Common, so I pedalled south along a very narrow twisting country lane and through the pretty little village of Horsley. Down eastwards, flat and straight parallel to Park Brook, in-between yellow fields of the ubiquitous buttercup, approaching the Rose and Crown cross-roads. Up the wooded Crown Hills and along through Smalley Common and down to the humble and tiny terraced house opposite Common Lane in the village of Stanley Common.

In the January of 1959 it was an unpleasant surprise to find that I was expected to attend my nearest school, the unknown Scargill Secondary Modern one mile to the east at West Hallam. The thought of being torn away from the cosy nest of Mother Cook and her brood of cheerful chicks was intolerable. I simply returned to Howitt and squatted at my rightful desk, defending my territory! Nothing was said and all was well. During the cold dark winter mornings it was well worth walking one mile west to the bus stop on the Derby - Heanor road at the Rose and Crown. There I stood and shivered until the elderly bus trundled along to collect a frozen and determined Howittian.

Huddling myself next to a murky misted window, the same cheerful pleasant conductor took my fare each dawn. Unknown to me then, this was Mr Christopher Dodsley, stepfather of Barry and Derek Goostrey. As March came in 'like a lion' and approached the 'out like a lamb' stage, my thoughts turned to cycling.

This, my fourteenth spring was the first, not only noticed, but completely embraced in the intoxication of delirious happiness. Adolescence is often associated with the discovery and pleasure of sex. In this I was no exception, but it should be remembered that all senses come of age, in that everything new and exciting feels good, tastes good, smells good and looks good. Each cycle ride to and from school was an adventure, and slightly different as the season advanced. The excellent sunny summer of 1959 started early in April and was still clinging to life in late warm October amid a blaze of colour. I savoured every moment of every day, watched the buds develop into bright green leaves, discerned flowers come and go, perceived the magnificent views to Crich Stand and the Derbyshire hills beyond. An embryonic deep love of our 'scept'red isle' developed, which would soundly defeat a later attempt to settle in an alien land. All this was orgasmic - in addition to the usual understanding of the word.

The morning ride out of the old mining village became more interesting as the distant westerly green patch work panorama opened out. To my left, fragrant nodding bluebells, a sea of colour from a fragment of the larger Morleyhayes wood. Turning north up to Smalley Green between thick thorny barriers of hawthorn, and occasional tangles of white flowered bramble. Singing his little heart out at the same spot each day, a spirited soaring skylark seemed to share my zest for life. Glimpses of glossy yellow celandine and patches of wood anemone flashed by before the leafy inviting Bell Lane appeared on the right. The pretty little Smalley Church set in its shady glade on the left just before Mr Crofts' house, and then I was speeding through the heart of Smalley Village. A curve to the east and on past Holly Mount Farm and rich Uncle Joe's handsome pre war prominent detached house on the right.

'Rich' by our standards. Joe Aldred, a man of few words, started his fortune sometime in the 1930's, by running a bus service from Heanor to Derby via Horsley Woodhouse, with my father Sam (1913-1972) and his brother, Arthur Annable (1905-1975) as drivers. He married Elizabeth Annable (1901-1962) my father's sister. Afterwards his empire extended into Derby including two ballrooms, the Ritz and the Rialto. He also had a garage and a TV/ radio shop on Normanton Road. The profits from all these enterprises supported a Rolls Royce and annual holidays on the French Riviera. It was frustrating when I eagerly asked the inarticulate Aunty 'lizabeth about these exotic experiences to get the same shy brief reply - *"Very nice"*.

Back on the bike I was entering Heanor, down the hill which had opencast mining on the left, now the site of Heanor Gate Comprehensive School. One of our group, William Havercroft lived on the right in one of the impressive homes in this sumptuous section of Heanor. Being opposite the scarred countryside, he was nicknamed 'Billy Outcrop'. Good natured and generous, I still treasure one of the most precious gifts ever given to me - the 45 rpm disc of Adam Faith singing 'Poor Me' on the 'A' side and the equally enjoyable 'The Reason' on the 'B' side. That record has given me nearly 40 years of great pleasure. Thanks Bill.

Past the old laundry on the left, up the hill and left again at the top into Nook End, right into Nelson Street and down past the home of the Goostrey's. Left into Park Street and right into Holmes Street at the end of which was William Howitt Secondary Modern School, and the completion of the four and a half mile journey. Cycles simply leaned against the wall, were never locked and no damage was ever inflicted. Unlike my comprehensive school, where the valuable property of those who braved the risk was locked inside a steel barred pen for the day. Even then there were frequent bouts of malicious vandalism.

There was much interest and excitement one day when Malcolm arrived on his shiny brand new BSA 'Golden Wings' 10 speed racer. Few of the lads could have afforded a bike of that calibre, let alone a new one. Even Mr Ferraby came out to join the throng of admirers.

Occasionally interesting and pleasurable distractions would delay me at school. Old films were sometimes shown in the canteen. I particularly remember at the end of one comedy starring Will Hay, when we tumbled out of the pre-fabricated effort in an ecstasy of joyous camaraderie giggles and fun! Raucous 'cheerio's' and 'see ya's' as I wheeled the bike ready to mount homeward bound. On this warm late spring evening the sun had already set leaving a gorgeous deep red to purple glow over Loscoe, and over Ilkeston there emerged a fat smiling orange moon as if to bestow a blessing upon the happy youth of Heanor. It was a fragrant journey in the growing darkness. Soon in open country with fields at either side, the multitudinous scents of meadowsweet, saxifrage, cowbane, cowparsley, hogweed, hemlock, yarrow, evening primrose, and the occasional nostalgic whiff of damp ramson, together with any number of roadside weeds. Growing coolness gave an exulted increase in energy as I stood rampant on pedals for greater power, acceleration, more and more speed through the balmy aromatic darkness. Such a blissful fleetness, unmeasurable and never exceeded since that enchanted ride which was more like flight!

Like all working people, over the years of school and jobs, there has always been the necessity, discipline, organisation and regimentation of getting out of bed and journeying to some location to earn a living each morning. As with Mundy Street Boys School and my last comprehensive school, I did not rise to the task with glee! However I can truthfully say that coming to consciousness each morning, during the two precious years of William Howitt Secondary Modern School; I could not wait to get on that bicycle to speed through the Derbyshire roads to my dear fun friends in Mrs Cook's classroom. Alas not all of her pupils entered the room with elation.

Terry Miles sat directly behind me. A ruminating lad whose good looks were spoilt by a constant scowl. In fact 'scowl' is the way he pronounced 'school' - spitting it out with contempt. His main aim in life was to get out of Mrs Cook's class and Howitt completely. Shortly before Easter 1960, I recall Mr Ferraby the woodwork teacher, pointing to Terry and saying -
"In two weeks time this will be the happiest lad in the world!".
Terry's attitude to school was reflected in the sad state of his work. In despair one day, Mrs Cook sent him to be formally reprimanded by Miss McLening. Grim faced she examined the sorry collection of scrawly, biscuit stained, dirty dog-eared examples of incorrect and incomplete work. *"These are **disgraceful!**"*

He had little interest, and less to say to the impish couple in front, but one conversation produced a stir.
"What's they gona do when tha gets out a 'scowl'?"

This addressed to Malcolm who made an unwise response -
"I might go to the Art School."
A sincere answer to what was a derisive question, but in the context of Heanor culture, it sounded haughty and pretentious giving Terry and his desk partner John Smith, hours of mimicry and mocking fun. For weeks to come we heard many guffaws in connection with poor Malcolm's - 'art scowl'.

In terms of fashion and good taste, Terry was a work of art himself. Unlike the slovenly baggy boys of today. Rightly proud of his smart stylish dress, we admired his 'Teddy Boy' trim well turned out look and frequent references to Mick Reed's. This was the Heanor house of fashion where natty young men would get fitted out in the latest Edwardian velvet collar coat, drainpipe trousers, bootlace ties and completing the trendy ensemble with fluorescent socks and 'brothel creeper' shoes of thick soft rubber soles. Michael Reed was located next door to where I used to live at Red Lion Square. My first ever suit came from there, inspired by a popular song called 'Mr Blue'. A made to measure bright azure garment with specified twelve inch bottoms! I reluctantly agreed to increase this last dimension by one inch, since the agitated tailor insisted they would defy all attempts to be put on!

Gathering information about these times, I re-united with my school friend Malcolm who looks almost the same as he did in the Howitt days! He commented on seeing my hair for the first time, free to roam and not plastered down with Brylcreem. Teenagers had a horror of dishevelled hair and like Kooky, (a vain character on TV) we were often seen catching a shop window reflection for a quick comb through. By the standards of the day, Terry Miles's hair was quite long. Nothing like the lengths of a decade later when Derek Goostrey looked like John Lennon, but long enough to attract comment from a sergeant - major style PE teacher. He took a disapproving look at Terry's 'mop', marched up very close and menacingly said -
"Am I hurting you lad?" "What d'ya mean Sir?"
"I should be. I'm treading on your hair!"

I have never admired sarcasm, but it is worth mentioning for the record that all staff were a good example in terms of dress and grooming. In the last comprehensive school before retirement, a male Head of Year

117

raised my conservative hackles by sporting a 'pony tail' and a male Head of PE wore an ear ring!

Terry Miles, who in these final years was just 'doing his time', had an eventful colourful past for one so young. References to these humorous escapades were once overheard by Mrs Cook. Off came the specs as the old lips wrinkled with censure - *"Just a minute! "Do you misbehave outside of school Terry Miles?"*

"No Miss." A simple response, but something in its terse comic quality caused the class to crack up. It took me nearly forty years to find out what our teacher had stumbled on. In 1957, a couple of twelve year olds had amused themselves by starting up a 22RB face shovel machine of the sort used in opencast work. The bucket rose up and smashed the cab! The result - a court case, in which Terry was seen as the less culpable party, but notwithstanding, boosted his infamous position in the eyes of the other boys in Loscoe Road School. He was a regular customer to the headmaster Mr Hubert Chambers, and the following is told of one of those visits. Having been caught smoking in the cloakroom by Mr Maurice Brentnall, Terry Miles and his mate Tony White (known as Nocca) were sent up to Mr Chambers 'for the stick'. They returned later grimacing, smarting, red faced, puffing on hands, muted mutterings and imprecations of recent pain. Such it was for those who transgress, and all present assumed that the law of the school had taken its just course. A crafty wink was exchanged between the disobedient duo and it emerged later that Mr Chambers knew nothing about secret smoking or a subsequent 'sticking'. Instead of ascending to the head's office, they returned to the cloakroom for a second smoke!

Corporal punishment was common practice in the 1950's. Belper's Mr Barlow, headmaster at Long Row Boys School, would walk into a suddenly silenced classroom grasping his long highly polished tortoiseshell cane between his two fists forming a flexing arch. Other teachers had shorter canes and some used them frequently for relatively minor offences. I often stood in a front of the class, involved in a public 'line of execution', as each hand was whacked in turn; and recall clearly the layers of old yellowing sellotape holding together the fraying end of the device - indicative of constant use!

The cane <u>was</u> used at William Howitt Secondary Modern School, but only by Mr Brentnall, very infrequently and always in private.

Personally I never saw it, or remember a single instance of usage. Derek Goostrey admits he was often hit by Mr Brentnall in the previous boys school, but in spite of all that, holds the man and his memory with great affection and in the highest esteem.

When I taught in St Bridget High School (1975-76) a tough private Catholic academy in Detroit, it was normal practice to use the 'paddle' on the bottoms of boys _and_ girls. The caretaker had the responsibility of making the paddles and it was customary for them to be inscribed with a name. To my embarrassment and disapproval he handed me "Big Daddy". It was not nice to hit kids. An unpleasant experience which disturbed me as much as the transgressor. Accordingly I do not mourn the passing of the cane, but deplore the progressive trend to avoid _any_ kind of punishment. They have made it very difficult to inflict even a small punishment. In my last comprehensive school, to put a miscreant on a half hour detention, one had to -

(1) Fill in an Incident Report explaining exactly what happened with full details of date, time, room etc.
(2) Go to the office and make copies of the above for - the Head of Humanities, Head of Year, Head of Department and the pupil's tutor.
(3) Complete a separate form for the Head of Humanities - giving similar information.
(4) Complete a similar form for the Head of Year.
(5) Provide work for the detention.

Frequently the worst offenders did not turn up to attend the punishment! After an exhausting day, when I am moving at a snail's pace, all this bureaucracy can take up to an hour - for a half hour detention! No wonder modern kids laugh at us.

The staff at Mundy Street Boys School and William Howitt Secondary Modern School only had to say - _"You will stay in!"_

A recent visit to see Terry Miles was sheer joy. Gone was the fresh faced skulking resentful scowl and in its place was friendly enthusiasm to reunite with an old classmate. Terry and his charming mother made me very welcome as we talked of old times. Interestingly he has absolutely no memory of Malcolm Caulton, but each time he uttered the word 'school' - it <u>still</u> sounded like 'scowl'! We were all in agreement that he was no angel, but one point was perfectly clear in our memory. At the roughest moments, Terry and similar difficult lads never forgot that the teacher was the boss and always treated with the utmost respect. It was ever *"Yes Sir / No Sir / Yes Miss / No Miss"*. Authority was never challenged, and none of us ever heard verbal abuse. Unlike modern pupils who are today encouraged to assert their 'rights', speaking to a member of staff forty years ago was deferential and <u>not</u> the same as speaking to another pupil.

Most experienced teachers will agree that the age of 13/14 tends to be the most difficult. We used to call them third years, but re-numbering them ninth years did not make them less bouncy, rumbustious or raucous. There came in Mrs Cook's class of third years, a dark day when a window was broken through boisterous behaviour. I can still see her face crumpling up in disapproval as she saw the shattered spectacle, before her gaze took note of our horrified faces. Only a fortnight later **another** pane was smashed by a different boy. Not to be offered as an excuse, but it should be pointed out that schoolroom glass, a la 1959, was thin and fragile. The second breakage in as many weeks produced a blasting reprimand which caused us all to be genuinely sorry for the situation. We were sincerely fond of our mistress and hated to see her so upset. Events were soon to prove that I had good cause to remember the warning, in the final words of her heated and dramatic rebuke - *"Let anyone else break a window!"*

It came to pass in those days that during break-time a group of pupils were in their glassy classroom enjoying a frolic. Usually the case with unsupervised adolescents. A certain Narvel Annable took it into his head to jump up to the heating pipe which followed the edge of the room above the windows. Thus enjoyably suspended, a certain Christine Thorpe took it into <u>her</u> head to pull on the boy's feet. She pulled the body out to an unstable angle and joyfully let go - resulting in a heavy pendulum swing which sent battering buttocks smashing into the shattering glass! I had to think very quickly, and to her credit, Christine decided to share responsibility. Enduring the long dreadful minutes before the end of 'playtime', finally a smiling Mrs Cook engrossed in pleasant animated conversation came bobbing through the door. Never did a countenance undergo such an extreme change from happy to incandescent rage in such

120

a speck of time. Glasses off, followed by - *"Just a minute....."* This was my cue to interpose and head off her attack.

"We'll pay for it. I have the money here and we'd like to
see the headmistress immediately to pay and apologise."

The Dame was successfully stopped in her tracks, and looked down doubtfully on my outstretched handful of small change. In fact large coins by the standards of the nineties. Several heavy copper old pennies with a few half pennies bearing the familiar sailing ship and one three-penny bit. More impressive was the silver including a sixpence and possibly even a shilling. To my certain memory was one big shiny half-crown. My generous mum gave me a good daily lunch allowance, but I doubt it covered the cost of the breakage. Moments later the lanky Christine, towering over her pimply partner in crime, and I were en route to the hallowed presence of Miss Mary McLening. All steeled up and ready to 'face the music', we were thwarted by a surprise reception from Mrs Cullen, the school secretary, who politely asked our urgent business and told us to wait outside until She within was ready to receive us. One simply did not get instant access to the Top Lady. In icy silence we suffered the miserable minutes in that cold corridor as I took another mournful look at the pittance in my grubby hand. Inside the inner sanctum, Miss McLening listened patiently as I enthusiastically released my prepared spiel, with Christine nodding and murmuring assent at suitable intervals.

The face of our headmistress was quite different to that of the old class teacher. At the age of 44, Mary McLening was still stunningly handsome and always very smart. From time to time my eyes were drawn from the attractive brown eyes to the beauty mole on her chin. Indeed those lovely eyes never stopped smiling behind the token sterness the occasion required. This charming gracious lady looked indulgently at the children before her and spoke a few firm words, mitigated by the consideration of the practical apology offered. She cordially refused my offering before we were given a regal dismissal. Bewitched, I was loath to leave. Back in the class room, the good natured gloating and sniggering were lost on my thoughtful introspection. Before the arrival of glaziers, the evidence of my deed was still there when Terry Sullivan returned after a short illness. Mindful of Mrs Cook's warning, he was aghast at noticing the airy opening and no doubt wondered who had been up for crucifixion. *"Arr Miss! Who's broken the window?"* She calmly responded with my name, but in so doing there was a twinkle in her eyes as they met mine, and a hint of smile around the lips.

A very different kind of window breaking took place at my last school more than 30 years later when nocturnal destructive pupils rampaged through the campus costing the rate payer hundreds of pounds each week during most of the term. After more than a month of this appalling vandalism, the headteacher was horrified at my suggestion of surveillance cameras, on the grounds that electronic spying would infringe the rights of the young culprits!

School Trip Venice 1961. At the front of the gondola is a pupil called Stan. The adults are - Keith Matthewman, Ian McIntyre, Vittorio Cirillo and Freda Brentnall.

Beryl Briggs, Mary McLening, Freda Brentnall & Anne Henshaw Brussels 1960.

Sports Day 1960. Keith Matthewman, Maureen Young and Anne Henshaw

122

A Gracious and Charming Headmistress

The broken window incident was not the only personal encounter I had with our headmistress. One morning a messenger was dispatched to Mrs Cook requiring certain people to attend the august presence. All pupils who were unable to go home at lunch time but did <u>not</u> eat a school dinner. In other words the daily chip shop and cafe brigade, comprising of a small group including the author. We were put under pressure to abandon our midday wandering habits and dine in the canteen. Miss McLening pointed out the good value of a nutritious subsidised meal - about a shilling (5p) at that time.

"Why would any of you want to walk <u>all</u> the way up to the
Market Place just for a greasy unwholesome chip?"

Up went my hand with typical adolescent indignation. I leapt at the opportunity of answering her rhetorical question. *"I get **choice**, Miss."*
There was much more than 'choice' to temp me to the Market Cafe on Godfrey Street, just south west of the Market Place. It was simply a civilised quiet place to dine with calm professional adults, but at thirteen, I lacked the ability to articulate these considerations to my headmistress. Passing the canteen each day, on hearing the clattering clamorous eaters within, I was grateful to exit into Allandale Road and lunch time freedom up the hill.

Back to 'choice', which was received like a slap. Miss McLening would not have taken kindly to such a response from her **staff**, let alone the impudent acned urchin in line. *"Oh!"* said She, lovely eyes blazing - *"What a pity it is not possible to go and check the canteen menu and walk out if it is not to 'sir's taste!!"* Silently standing sensing being on very firm ground - I stood my ground, savouring the point scored. On dismissal, walking back to the home room, proud smiles quietly cheered me a hero. Further eminence came from, of all people, David Martin who repeated the little drama to our teacher - who, of course supported the management line.

A part of me was sad to have annoyed the lady who had become a goddess. With sincere penance, decades later, I can offer to my esteemed Lady, all the miserable school meals forced down in harsh emotional indigestible conditions during the years of midday comprehensive cacophony. Even if not officially on duty, an eating member of staff is (de facto) on duty! You cannot ignore the bad behaviour of the 'pigging in' pupils on the next table or indeed any table.

Horace Hart enjoyed the school dinners and said - *"It was a real treat!"*

Pam Carter told me that the rules of the Heanor Grammar School were very clear in the early 1950's. *"We were about 500 strong, and Mr Egner the headmaster knew every one of us. You would not **dare** do wrong. He knew what you were doing in and out of school! The prefects were watching and reporting. At midday you wore your hat and didn't eat in the street. No visits to the chip shop, Milk Bar or wandering around the town. You either stayed for a school dinner or went home. It was as clear cut as that!*

Malcolm who sometimes dined in the canteen told me that on a few occasions he found to his horror, a living slug on his plate from the poorly washed lettuce! Unlike my five shillings a day, his allowance was just enough to cover the cost of five school lunches - five shillings a week. After this appalling slimy molluscous experience, he joined me at the Market Cafe as often as funds would stretch, usually Monday and Tuesday. The much vaunted 'choice' consisted of various items on toast. Beans, egg, sardines etc., usually at 1/6 (7.5p). Something and chips went in to the two shilling mark. A cup of tea was three pence. Best value was the three course set lunch at 4/-, (20p) which we considered too expensive and uninteresting. During the dinner times of Wednesday through Friday, Malcolm starved - but for the odd bar of chocolate consumed at the house of 'Billy Outcrop'. An interesting place to spend lunch, since the large garden included a fish pond and aviary.

The Market Cafe was in two halves. To the right was the snack bar with juke box and to the left a quieter dining room for meals. Above the clatter of pots, cutlery, comings, goings and hum of conversation; I could still enjoy the melodic strains travelling across the

124

two rooms and central corridor from that space aged, push buttoned chrome and gaudily illuminated cabinet called the 'juke box'. As a totally biased opinion, the charts of 1959 have never been equalled for the sheer joy of talented excellence. Most of them were winners and are occasionally heard today with nostalgic reverence. They are particularly meaningful to our generation since the lush orchestration combined with a boyish voice, catharsised and encapsulated our fresh green hopes, dreams and fantasies.

One day I was entranced by what seemed like a sweet sounding choir of angels ascending and descending the scale, complemented by a resonant twangy bass guitar. Into this euphonious mix came, exactly at the right time, a deep masculine voice with just a hint of the sexy adolescent croak so typical of this new young genre. He could easily have been mistaken for Elvis, but these dulcet notes were a touch lighter, and for my taste, with great respect to the King - better. This sensuous singer had composed both music and lyrics of this beautiful work which lasted barely more than a precious two minutes. After such an orgasmic audible experience, in complete contrast to the hateful pious dirges of just a stone's throw away; this new music now became an important part of my life. In the following few weeks, almost each day, I struggled to hang on to the illusive hypnotic notes of the same record above the ambient din of the busy Market Cafe. A few occasional discernible words -
"...and in the evening, by the moonlight..."
I knew not the name of the singer or 45 rpm cover, to be able to ask for it in the record shop. A pointless exercise not possessing a player, let alone the expensive seven shillings to purchase. Eventually the time came when I held the precious seven inch vinyl disc, with its grooved integral encoded magical music, bearing the legend -
"Maybe Tomorrow".
Later, examining the sleeve of a prize long playing record, I peered long and hard into the stunningly handsome features of my teenage idol
Billy Fury.

One day at school, Miss McLening announced an optional official uniform - grey trousers and a black blazer. Terry Miles recoiled in horror and firm refusal, as I did myself, and a few fashion conscious others. Valerie Billett recalls that most pupils did in fact comply.

125

Some mavericks including those high in the pecking order - Hutchinson / Grace / Lambert / Martin and others from the westerly villages of Smalley and Horsley Woodhouse; dared to arrive in bright red jeans! It is unclear how Miss McLening dealt with this.

An Image of Popular Culture. Billy Fury was born on April 17th, 1941 and died at the age of 41 on January 28th 1983. His real name was Ronald Wycherley. This picture (origin unknown) was extracted from a scrapbook.

In the wider area of South Derbyshire, Heanor is regarded as a rough earthy town, so it was interesting to note how most of my Heanor contributors recall the lads from the out of town villages as being more wayward and rebellious. Diplomatically put by Miss Brentnall as -
"Colourful characters and likeable amusing rouges!"

126

This comment intrigued me since my family are from Horsley Woodhouse.

After the Mundy Street dark grey morning gatherings, the McLening morning assemblies were by contrast rather like the aforementioned jeans - bright red and cheery. The hymns were far more acceptable, encouraging and even nostalgic -
> *"All things bright and beautiful"*, and better still -
> *"Glad that I live am I, that the sky is blue.*
> *Glad for the country lanes and the fall of dew.*
> *After the sun the rain, after the rain the sun...."*

These frequently sung much loved lines lifted the spirits and seem to underline my new found joy of nature. The latter was possibly one of her favourites and apt for the time. It **was** good to be alive in 1959 at Howitt, and the sky **was** indeed blue. I gather both the above had been condemned as 'politically incorrect' and consequently banned in schools today. Yet another example of the progressive Mafia and the power they still wield.

Valerie Hodson nee Billett, called affectionately in those days 'Bullet', was the Head Girl for the two years of 1958 to 1960. It all came back to me when I heard the same efficient slightly formal clipped voice talking about hymn and prayer books. They were supposed to be taken to each assembly but sometimes forgotten.
"Being the big fourth years standing right at the back, we hoped to conceal the lack of hymn books, and were singing along anyway. Occasionally Mr Brentnall would spot this pretence of following invisible lines and give us a roasting!"

I recall a morning when Miss McLening left the hall suddenly after starting a coughing fit. Mr Brentnall quickly took her place, but we were genuinely concerned over this ominous incident. Four decades later Miss Briggs explained -
> *"She struggled with poor health and was under treatment*
> *from a specialist in Derby for chronic and severe asthma."*

On Friday the headmistress called for the grand total of house points when each of the four house captains would go up, use the flat of the chalk for size, and boldly inscribe the final figure on the blackboard. In an age when regular competition was acceptable, we all looked forward

127

to see which team had come top. Would it be Chatsworth (green) Wingfield (red) Flamstead (blue) or Dale (yellow) - my own team? During the following year when I had been promoted into Mr Brentnall's class, Miss McLening surprised us once by making a critical comment on the inflationary impressive totals which were now well into the low hundreds.

*"With these figures, some of you must be getting house points in tens at a time! Staff are reminded that they should be awarded **sparingly** and only for exceptional achievement."*

Perhaps I remember this because it was so unusual for pupils to hear a public staff reprimand, be it ever so gentle. Mr Brentnall did not take it too gently when he sharply addressed us back in the classroom.

"Where are all these house points coming from then?"

We looked at each other doubtfully before Carol Bestwick hesitantly spoke - *"Mrs Buxcey"*. It was indeed uncharacteristically generous of the strict squat little history teacher to give several house points on the rare occasions she gave them at all.

Miss Freda Brentnall, the Howitt games mistress, is today Mrs Freda Cirillo and has been kind enough to give me an insight into the character of Miss Mary McLening.

"She could be very firm indeed, was strict with pupils <u>and</u> staff, running a 'tight ship'. Some teachers became very upset when reprimanded."

To my great surprise this type of comment was supported by others who well remember the headmistress. I came to this project with a bias willing to hear nothing but good and light of my captivating Lady; and equally willing to hear bad and dark of the 'demon headmaster' up the hill! One male member of staff had told me that she had a tendency to be more strict and distant with the masters, and had better relations and a closer affinity to the mistresses. On the other hand a mistress who had worked at the school for a short time said the opposite was true! Miss Brentnall pointed out that men do not like to be told off by a woman, especially in those days before male authority had been eroded by the feminist movement a decade later.

"She was the captain of her ship and you toed the line! At our staff meetings people were sometimes afraid to speak. She could put you down and some of us felt very small indeed, especially the men! Lesson

plans and record books were checked and signed weekly. Some staff were infuriated by a red line through, and 'Sp' next to a spelling error.

Miss Beryl Briggs was a close friend of Miss McLening for many years and well acquainted with the character. Before she was appointed Senior Mistress at Aldercar Secondary Modern School in 1955, Miss Briggs served under her friend at the Loscoe Road Girls School as the art mistress.

"She was great! Affectionately referred to as 'Mac'. Warm, charming and generous, yet these qualities were mixed with firmness."
She went on to tell me of another friend, a 'good teacher', who had to leave the school after just a few months because -
"She could not get along with Mac at all! Just didn't make the grade."
Mary Holmes nee Watson said -
"Miss Mary McLening was my very first headmistress in September 1956 after leaving college. I was in awe of her!
A fascinating picture was beginning to form of this interesting and complex lady. Miss Brentnall, after a few prickly episodes, eventually became very fond of Mac. In 1954 the young Freda walked onto the campus and asked a *"frumpy woman"* the way to Miss McLening's office. It was the headteacher herself! She became slimmer and smarter by the time Howitt was born four years later. This theme of improvement was echoed by Joyce Clay nee Sumner, who was a pupil in the late 1940's. *"When we saw Miss McLening years later at re-unions she actually looked **younger** than when we were at school!"* She had a high standard of dress, very smart, clean and tidy - not like the teachers of today.

On one occasion, teacher and headteacher were in conference when a child gave Freda a short message. *"Oh yes, right oh."* *"Really Miss Brentnall! 'Right oh', - **much** too familiar and what kind of grammar is that to set an example?"*
Poor Freda wondered if she was one of the first of the generation to let standards slip to the appalling depths which we have plumbed today.

This affirmation of standards puts me in mind of an incident a few years later. Derek Limer had a few minutes of friendly and informal chat to one of his teachers on a public bus and reaching his stop said -
"Cheerio Sir." At his Derby school the next day, he was hauled in

front of the class and reprimanded for an inappropriate way to leave a master. *"Good evening Sir"* would have been correct. Here in the 1990's after thirty years of liberal progressive education, that same strict teacher sharing public transport with his pupils would be at risk of receiving a mouth full of verbal abuse!

The professional relationship between Miss Brentnall and Miss Mary McLening matured with increasing friendship over the years.
"Whatever criticism she came up with, I always had an answer.
When you stood up to her she'd back off. No surrender for me!"
There speaks the firm confident efficient freckled Miss Brentnall we all knew and loved. Most of the time she was recalled energetically shepherding a group of girls to some practice, equipped with a whistle around her neck, wearing sexy little shorts. At this sight a ripple of excitement went through the adolescent boys. Derek Goostrey looks back fondly on 'her good legs'. She threw us a quick glance, half smile and warning glint which seemed to say -
*"Desirable I may be, but don't forget - I am **still** the teacher!*

Miss Brentnall was proud of her girls who won a netball trophy.
"Glenis Whelan could throw the ball right across the court!"

At one stage she taught us English and once lent me a pen. I was typical of the adolescent who is occasionally forgetful and disorganised. Later as a teacher I quickly learned <u>not</u> to supply pens. Pupils came to rely on the hand out, and they were seldom returned. A 'no pen policy', backed up by the threat of punishment, soon produced a responsible well equipped class. Miss Brentnall did get her biro back, but I am ashamed to say it was damaged due to abuse. I still cringe at the look she gave me at the end of that class.

She gave Derek Goostrey a much sweeter look, when by mistake he addressed her as 'Mum', and promptly went a deep shade of red amidst uproarious laughter. She quickly quelled the carnival by gently patting him on the head and said -
"He can call me 'Mum' anytime".

Referring to the recent Howitt re-unions, Freda told me how surprised she was by receiving hugs and kisses from enthusiastic and affectionate ex-pupils. No surprise at all to the rest of us! We all have happy memories of dancing the Veleta to the crackly sound of Harry

130

Davidson and his Orchestra in the canteen room. In those frenetic but enjoyable high days of 'Rock n' Roll', Miss Brentnall is to be thanked for bringing a little charm and grace into our brash adolescent lives.

Mary Holmes said -
*"To have Miss McLening as your first head directly after college was a valuable experience. She insisted on correct lesson planning for **every** lesson to include aims, objectives and suitable follow up work. This work was inspected in your record book **every** week, sometimes with comment and always signed. She was a strict disciplinarian, but if you did your job properly, there was no kinder, more understanding, more helpful person. If you did right by her - then she was wonderful."*

Unfortunately this level of guidance and structure for beginning modern teachers is unfashionable today. On the plans of one RE lesson, Miss Watson had carefully explained five main parts. Miss McLening wrote down a number six -
"I have some pictures which you may borrow
if you would like to show them to the class."
An example of how she would look after you and put a young teacher on the right path. On one occasion the conscientious but inexperienced Mary Watson was saved from the wrath of the caretaker. A lesson involving clay had made a mess, and the next morning he was waiting for her at the classroom ready with bitter recriminations about all the extra work she had caused! By chance the headmistress was passing, overheard the ensuing reprimand and took pity on the probationer quivering in her shoes. She interceded, asserted her authority making it clear that Miss Watson needed to do her job. At the same time the caretaker was soothed with assurances that in future, all efforts would be made to leave the class in a reasonable condition.

I cheered long and loud when Freda Cirillo recalled Miss McLening becoming angry with an interfering advisor from County Hall and ordered him off the premises!
*"This is **my** school and I will stick to the tried and tested.*
GET OUT!!"

How I wish it would have been possible for me to say the same thing to an over paid left wing progressive advisor, who in the 1990's put me under great pressure to arrange my class into groups with collective rather than individual responsibility, tolerate more noise and stop frequent testing. Against the international background of our falling educational standards, the progressives have much to answer for. According to the Sunday Times, October 5th 1997, Britain ranks 32nd out of 53 countries for the quality of its primary and secondary education system. Also our 13 and 14 year olds are the equivalent of one year's education behind most other European countries, and even further behind Japan - where a 'McLening' style classroom is still the norm.

It was indeed a sad day for education in July 1975 when Miss Mary McLening retired.
She was born at Oldham in 1915, and gained her qualifications at Lincoln Teacher Training College. She became the head of Loscoe Road Girls School in January 1948, a headship which was to last 28 years, one year longer than the tenure of Mr Leonard Smith, and three years shorter than her predecessor.

In her first log entry Miss Mary McLening generously honours the departing Miss Winifred A Westland, whose term spanned four decades and two World Wars. In so doing, I believe she was also defining her own professional objectives for the coming years. Objectives which I know from personal experience, she achieved.
"After many years of faithful and intelligent service in this school, the headmistress in now retiring. She leaves the school in a good condition of efficiency with substantial assets in the way of attainments and discipline, and regard for those finer points which always distinguish a good girls school. Excellent sport has been forthcoming from loyal and competent staff who obviously have spared no pains to make their work effective. The school can be described as a happy one with a markedly good tone and influence. The approaching completion of the standard huts should allow of more progress being made since the retiring headmistress has laid such an excellent foundation of habits and attainments.
Her successor therefore comes into a fortunate inheritance."

One of those 'standard huts' would eventually become the happy classroom of dear old Mrs Cook.

In July 1964 William Howitt Secondary Modern School was no more - after a short but effective and eventful life of just six years. Since Heanor Gate, a major project, must have been in the planning stage for at least as many years, one is given to wonder if Howitt was **intended** to have a short life, a stop gap in readiness for the new big comprehensive school.

This is where I can claim to share the significance of a career spell involving seventeen years. My period at the comprehensive school and Miss McLening as head at Loscoe Road School. She was offered a deputy headship at Heanor Gate Comprehensive School, but said -

"No! I've been seventeen years running my own school. To accept the offer would amount to an effective demotion. I'll stay at Howitt."

At the new William Howitt Junior Community School she stayed until her retirement eleven years later when she reached the age of 60. After such a splendid career everyone expected her to have a long and well earned retirement. Sadly this was not to be the case.

Two days before the assassination of President Kennedy in 1963, the close friends Mary McLening and Beryl Briggs had a house built, designed in two parts to give each lady independence, privacy, economy, and at the same time convenience for long term good companions. Into retirement the ex-colleagues had jointly purchased a bungalow in Denia on the south coast of Spain in the Province of Alicante, for the enjoyment of annual holidays. They were driving in this area on their way to visit some local friends in 1977. Seat-belts had not long been introduced at that time. Mac and Beryl had, in sunny carefree fashion, discussed the pros and cons of the new safety device. The former friend was far seeing and keen, but the latter, not liking to be tied in, took a more sceptical view. Miss Briggs related the horrific events of that tragic day.

"We were happily driving along when suddenly a car came whizzing around a corner and hit us head on! It was a young Frenchman and his wife on their honeymoon. We were both hurt, but Mac's seat belt had badly cut into her chest. No doubt without the restraint, she'd have gone flying through the windscreen with even more devastating results."

133

The two injured friends were taken to a private clinic where they shared the same ward. After an x-ray, it was decided to operate on Miss Mary McLening overnight. She did not survive.

Here was laid to rest, our Queen of Howitt, who reigned over a brief 'Camelot' creating a magical and happy period for the author and many others; ending her very successful life at the age of 62. I speak for many Howittians when expressing genuine affection and love for the woman who filled the school with sunshine. Love! This is the one word which keeps re-occurring. The love of this special lady must have permeated the very fabric of the building and hallowed the ground.

Mary McLening, like Princess Diana was one of 20 million victims to die a violent death on the roads in the hundred years since the first fatal car accident in 1898. Polly Toynbee, writing in the Radio Times, 8.1.98., put the ever present danger into perspective -

"Most people under 50 know someone who has died in a car,
but no one who's died in a war."

Miss Briggs showed me a last precious photograph of her sadly missed dear Mac. I was unprepared to view this picture which gave me the same kind of emotional experience as when I gazed at a 99 year old portrait of my very first teacher, the formidable Miss Florence Calder. The Belper dame was recalled as ancient and deeply wrinkled, but here was Florence an attractive young girl of 22.

In the case of Miss Mary McLening, it was the opposite. I recalled a smart dignified woman, if over forty, glowing with benign beautiful features. This is how she was, frozen, in that split moment of time, 38 summers and springs back, forever standing next to Derek Goostrey holding his 'Double Diamond' tray. Common sense should have told me that the Miss McLening more than 20 years on could not have maintained that mystical magnificence. The image of the older woman, unrecognisable at first glance, grey and bonny, far from Heanor, enjoying the sun of an alien land was somehow - disturbing.

A Kind and Cosy Motherly Teacher

Miss McLening very nearly did <u>not</u> get onto the aforementioned Easter photograph of Mr Maurice Brentnall's class. As we were all posed she just happened to be passing on the way to her office when Mr Brentnall casually called over in his typical relaxed friendly way -

"Are you coming into the photograph Miss McLening?"
Thinking this an excellent idea, a chorus of the girls enthusiastically urged - *"Yes!! Come on Miss! Come on! Come on!*

For a moment I feared she would refuse, but under tremendous pupil pressure the elegant besuited mistress reluctantly, but kindly stood with us to produce a picture which has become one of my most precious possessions. For nearly forty years I thought Derek Goostrey was <u>told</u> to hold his beer tray, so that 'Howitt Secondary 1960' could be written upon it. Not so! He did it for sheer devilment! The school name and date was added to attempt an obliteration of the well known boozy advert.

"I got a right rollicking from Moggy Brentnall for that!"
This prank may not have 'worked wonders' for Derek at that time, but in retrospect it was a portentous pointer to one of his favourite future pastimes! Centre front stands sexy Dennis Aistrop with typical tilted head and confident cocky bearing. A jauntiness which captures the exciting optimistic mood of the time. Just above his head and to the right is Maureen Hall who sadly died of cancer at the age of 23. Apart from Maureen and the headmistress, to the best of my knowledge, the rest of us are all still alive.

Mr Crofts paid tribute to the services of John Lavender, the lad on the top row extreme right. A competent technician who assisted the science master on many occasions with electrical equipment and particularly as the school projectionist. From experience I know the value of a reliable pupil to have the skill to operate the old style film projector when it is necessary for a teacher to watch and control the class. Not so much a problem today with the simplified Video/TV equipment. At St Bridget High School in Detroit, I recall with gratitude

Mr Maurice Brentnall's 'A' Class, Easter 1960

Top Row - Narvel Annable, Graham Waterall, Michael Annable, Keith Harbon, Michael Fletcher, Glyn Parker, Don Sloman and John Lavender. *Third Row* - Glenis Whelan, Christine Scott, Oriel Brown, Valerie Billett, Barbara Brown, Enid Bull and Carol Bestwick. *Second Row* - Sylvia George, Josephine Vallance, Janice Marriott, Maureen Hall, Joan Meakin, Anne Boxall and partly hidden behind Mr Brentnall is Marline Saxton. *Front Row* - Miss Mary McLening (headmistress), Derek Goostrey holding his 'Double Diamond' tray, Mick Sims, Denis Aistrop, Trevor Brown and Mr Maurice Brentnall.

136

my own projectionist who was known as Ricky. Incidentally, his real name was Horace Harrell.

This was not Mrs Cook's class and <u>not</u> the class I wanted to be in after the six weeks holiday of summer 1959. At the 'end of year' exams in her remedial group, I beat the competition and came top of the class; boosting my confidence, but totally unaware of the personal disaster this Pyrrhic triumph would bring down upon my head. It was still hot and sunny in September 1959, for this my last precious year at Howitt in the top fourth year. Chickenpox, a confounded nuisance, delayed my eager start to the autumn term by a fortnight, and I was bemused to be put into the adjacent prefabricated classroom, which only weeks before had been occupied by the much lusted after and attractive Miss Olive Walker.
The young lady had gone, and this was now Mr Maurice Brentnall's fourth year 'A' class! It gradually sank in that my promotion was so steep and dramatic that I had 'over shot' the 'B' group now taught by Mr Rigby in one of the old rooms. There is a huge difference between the atmosphere of a low ability class and the very top class. All was now quieter, more conservative, conscientious and serious. I would have loved it as Mr Annable the teacher, but hated it as Narvel Annable the mischievous adolescent, who had just experienced the most fun packed year of his life giggling at Malcolm's naughty cartoons and generally enjoying the ongoing circus around him. During the first wood work lesson Mr Ferraby said -
"You've got away from that lot now and
can get down to some serious work."
But I was sad, and wanted to be back with my boisterous bouncy friends and beloved dear old Mrs Cook. Poor Mrs Cook, the fun was often at her expense. Like the time she tried to read us a poem and never got past the first line! David broke his pencil, Sos fell off his chair, Pearl was going to tell her Aunty Rosie about somebody who had just upset her, Terry Miles was muttering 'scowl' and what a waste of time it all was, Billy had said something to make Sandra furious, Terry Sullivan dropped a pen, and Jessie was bitterly complaining that her unflattering nickname from the Caulton/Annable duo had been elongated into an even more offensive appellation!
"Just a minute!" came several times, and
we never <u>did</u> hear the rest of that poem.

Perhaps the author's strict boy/girl seating plan of some twenty years on may have helped. A Narvel sitting next to Pearl at the front of the room would have been well sobered and reduce his chronic hysterics. A Malcolm sat at the back of the room next to Jessie would have reduced his roguish artistic ardour.

It all became too much for her on one occasion when she kept us in after school to write a composition. Her idea of an unpleasant task, but as you see, I have always enjoyed writing. This lady was loved and there was an air of genuine sadness that she had been moved to take such an unusual extreme measure. She had threatened us with the information that it was not necessary for her to teach. Her husband, Mr Percy Ward Cook (1896 - 1980) had a prosperous business of a garage in Smalley and one in Heanor. After about ten minutes somebody asked how long we would be delayed. She sensibly ignored the question, screwed her face up into its fiercest grimace and simply reminded us of why we were being punished. At that moment a cleaning lady walked by the room on the side path, and caught our teacher's eye. Mrs Cook being a polite sociable and popular woman, had to suddenly unscrew her face into a charming friendly smile of acknowledgement for barely a second before a dramatic return to grim disapproval.

Unfortunately we were tickled by this dramatic and abrupt transformation, to the point of Brenda McKay laughing out loud. This enraged the already angry mistress who screwed up her wrinkly lips further to a deep grimace, piercing poor Brenda with furious bespectacled eyes. Brenda went red. Some minutes later the headmistress passed by and noticed the silent class still in session. She came in and whispered something to Mrs Cook, who returned the whisper. Five years later I discovered the nature of that whispered exchange. I was living in the US and on an eventful and extended holiday in Britain, when I visited my revered old teacher in Hardy Barn, at her impressive home set on three quarters of an acre with lovely views across Shipley. She gave me a sad tired forgiving smile when I apologised for the trouble we had been to her, and spoke of the unexpected visit to the impromptu detention and hushed conversation with Miss McLening.

Miss McLening - *"Why are you keeping them in?"*

Mrs Cook - *"Misbehaviour - of course!"*
Miss McLening - *"You're not supposed to. Some of these pupils have already missed their bus back to Smalley and Horsley Woodhouse."*
Mrs Cook (now angry) - *"Miss McLening! You tell **me** - HOW am I supposed to discipline this class!*

Needless to say my sympathies are entirely with the teacher. This would be the embryonic beginning of the bureaucracy which was to tie the hands of teachers and allow two generations to get out of control. I have no memory of any formal procedure for detention or of any letters sent home. It was simply a case of 'You will stay in', and in we would stay until such time as it pleased the mistress or master to release us. Freda Cirillo put the decline of the last 60 years very well -
*"When I was at school in the 1940's it was common practice to be given **further** punishment at home, if it was discovered you had annoyed a teacher. If a ruler dropped onto the floor at Howitt, half a dozen pupils would rush to pick it up. At a typical school today, half a dozen pupils would walk over it!"*

One day a new teacher came in and received our undivided attention. He gave us a 'one off' history lesson and never came back to our particular class. Mr Keith Matthewman was a good looking, erudite, sophisticated, gentle, young man. After entering, a respectful silence descended, a silence born of the unknown. He had a presence which might have made us 'be upstanding', except that it was not the custom at William Howitt Secondary Modern School. It was, as if some future inaudible voice had said - 'Silence in Court'!

He captured our interest immediately by speaking on the subject of Victorian morality and standards. You could have heard a pin drop. There was no fiddling or fidgeting as we heard about the strict separation of boys and girls some 80 years back. We leaned forward and hung onto every word of his careful measured delivery as he introduced us to the term 'chastity belt'. This came from the word 'chaste', meaning **no** sex, purity, abstinence - paws OFF! I gave Malcolm a quick impish grin who quite rightly nudged me to pay attention. He wanted to hear more. The chastity belt, made of strong leather, was secured in place around the nether forbidden regions of a maiden with a pad lock. Sort of 'lock up knickers'. The key to this perceived spoil sport device, hung around the neck of a grim faced

139

mother, who accompanied her untrusted and potentially wayward daughter to the lavatory.

"There she stood sentry whilst nature took its necessary course.
Afterwards the girl was re-locked before joining the others!"

Over the years since Mr Matthewman's memorable lesson, I have often cogitated on the folly of giving boys a challenge. For days afterwards there was much fascination and naughty comment on the subject of picking locks. Malcolm drew a side-splitting cartoon of a frowning unyielding Mrs Buxcey, handing out chastity belts to all the puzzled girls in her class. Sad faced boys eyeing a large master key securely hanging around her neck.

Mr Matthewman was amused at my memory and interpretation of the long lost lesson, which was a little different to his original lecture forty years before. Our recollection correctly captures the attitude of Victorian men to their women, but in fact the infamous 'belt' was an ugly medieval device used by untrusting soldiers who locked up their wives before they went off to war!

It was a great joy to discover that a prestigious observer such as Keith Matthewman, shares my idyllic rosy reminiscence of William Howitt Secondary Modern School.

"After my previous appointment, Howitt was a happy experience. The all boys secondary school at Barking, East London was tough. Morning assembly consisted of hymns and canings. The regime was hard and disciplined, and had to be in a London all boys school. Caning was the normal punishment for wrong doing, but the fact was - caned boys did not come back for more! On the other hand I have no doubt, (and my experience at Howitt confirmed this) that the civilising presence and influence of girls makes corporal punishment unnecessary.

He went on to say that he got on very well with Miss McLening.

"She was a splendid headmistress who had created the chemistry of a relaxed helpful atmosphere. Co-education had a civilising influence on school life. Howitt had a liveliness which I enjoyed. People knew how to be courteous and how to be kind. It was similar to my own happy days as a pupil at Long Eaton Grammar School."

Mr Matthewman had a short career as a teacher, but it was worth while. *"In my whole career, either at the Bar or on the Bench, I have never had any moments happier than in teaching young people. At the end of a school day there is no more satisfying experience than to find that the kids have learned something. Winning an unwinable case in court does not come higher on the scale of satisfaction."*

You will have gathered that Mr Matthewman is now His Honour Judge Keith Matthewman Q.C. of the Nottingham Crown Court. So it is just as well that Mrs Cook's class behaved themselves on that day!

Mr Matthewman found Mrs Cook - *"Homely, pleasant helpful and kind"*. As did Mary Watson in her first job, who was greatly helped by the older experienced teacher.

"She was in the next classroom and was most kind, such as showing me how to take the register. Mrs Cook generated warmth. You could feel comfortable with her. The sort of person everybody would love to have as a mother."

"The sort of person everybody would love to have as a mother."

Miss Watson's last line struck a chord. I fully agreed, and yet this utterance became highly significant when I visited the home of Mr Barry Cook her son, in October 1997.

I was made very welcome by Mr and Mrs Kathleen Cook, who were keen to help me honour the lady who had given me the confidence and encouragement to graduate from a group of slow learners up to the level of a university degree in little more than a decade. They listened politely as I poured out love and affection for this esteemed patient gentle little lady. What followed was a surprise. They were in full agreement that Mrs Doris Cook was an excellent teacher -

"My mother was a schoolteacher 100% - totally committed. Every part of her life revolved around the school. Her conversation was school. Her friends were teachers. She lived for school. Spare time was taken up with Sunday School. She was a teacher first - a mother second."

By teaching standards of the day Mrs Cook did not come across as a strong disciplinarian. For the most part she was approachable, warm and understanding. After Mundy Street, my daily trips to Howitt were more like a visit to 'granny's house', but this was at variance to the experience of her son. I said that she never hit any of us.

*"No - she saved **that** for me! Mother believed in an old fashioned slap. It's a wonder my ears aren't twice the size with all the clouting they had!"*

Mrs Kathleen Cook continued - *"She was very strict with Barry, to the point of locking him up in his bedroom. He once escaped by climbing out of the window! Things would get so bad that he went to stay with his aunt at the blacksmith's shop in Brinsley, to keep out of her way!"*

Mrs Doris Cook took an enthusiastic and heavy handed interest in the education of her son -

"First question after school - 'Do you have any homework?' I'd say 'Yes, plenty'. 'Are you sure?' She would inspect my books and set more work if necessary. I never got out! It was a privilege to have a private education at Stainsby Hall school which I left in 1951. I know she made sacrifices for me and did her best, but by nature I am more practical than academic. She thought the world of my cousin who did well in exams and continually made unfavourable comparisons, yet he couldn't knock a nail into a piece of wood!"

This last intrigued me because I had suffered the same experience in reverse. Sam Annable occasionally expressed disappointment in the son who, could not mend his bike or repair a puncture, could not kick a ball or show any manly interest in sport. Unfortunately for me, practical incompetence was <u>not</u> balanced by academic achievement at school. *"What **can** you do?"*

It would seem that Mrs Doris Cook like the author shared a strong respect and veneration for all things academic. Her school diary and meetings took precedence over family outings or even holidays. Barry's girlfriends were quizzed about their job, school background and qualifications for suitability as an erudite future daughter-in-law. In later years even her granddaughter Tracy was given extra homework which, led, sadly, to infrequent visits.

Fascination of this complicated and contradictory woman grew. As we waded through the memorabilia and old photographs it became clear that in spite of the frank revelations, Barry Cook was very proud of his multi talented and popular mother.

"Each Christmas she received loads and loads of cards."

In retirement she worked hard for the Women's Institute as their president, and was heavily involved with the Church. The building no longer exists, but her father was a founder member of the Methodist Church of Christ at Underwood in Palmerston Street. Doris Cook was very busy with the anniversary, competitions and even elocution lessons.

"She was a marvellous cook making beautiful cakes and pastry."

Her energetic artistic side came out in flower arranging and dress making. Like the author she loved to visit local gardens, but unlike the author, was a keen hard worker in her own well tended garden. Her son gave this amusing retrospection -

"After her retirement I had a granny flat built onto the Hardy Barn house, and we moved in with my ageing parents to be close and able to look after them. Many is the time we would see mother slowly - painfully, struggling up the garden, laden with two over full buckets of weeds. Stopping now and again, panting out of breath, head shaking sorrowfully under the burden of her heavy toil."

This picture of drudgery, sweat and slog was sometimes seen by guests, and it looked as if the poor little old lady was left to maintain the large garden all by herself.

"Not so! She was such an ardent worker insisting on personally performing these daily chores to achieve a weed free colourful display. With friends looking on it was embarrassing, but I could predict every stage of this labour. 'Watch now, she's putting the buckets down. Now comes the heart-rending shaking of the head - there you are! Didn't I tell you!!'"

Mrs Doris Cook began life in Underwood Nottinghamshire, on December 22nd 1902 as Doris Higton. Her university years at Leeds were from 1922 to 1926 when she specialised in maths. What a treat to see the young gay abandoned frolicking Doris with her fellow students in an old photograph. Only a few years on from the restrictions of Victorian fashion. Here are the shades of the boyish straight lines of the day, flat chests and scandalous short skirts revealing the calves of legs. Looking at naughty Doris and her three 'flappers', one can almost hear - 'Charleston! Charleston!' The voluminous bushy white hair of old age is here in its original form, parted in the same place, strong wild and black. I wonder what became of her fun loving friends?

Mrs Doris Cook in Early Days

The young frolicking Doris at Leeds University in the early 1920's with her college friends. The seaside photographs of 1937 show Mr Percy Ward Cook, Mother Cook and young Barry.

One photograph showed her father highly decorated, who appeared to be wearing mayoral chains. Mr Higton was a member of the Ancient Order of Foresters. He was a secretary by day, and a barber in the evenings. As the big butch gruff growling miners came in for their twice weekly shave, little young Doris had the job

of lathering their faces all ready for her dad to use his cut-throat razor.
"Mek a good job on it lass!"

Each collier had his own decorated personal shaving mug, which stayed in the shop and was lined up on the shelf in neat rows with the others. In coal mining communities Doris's job was usually done by boys called 'lather-lads'.

On October 8th 1931 she married Percy Ward Cook at Underwood Church. She was 29 and he 35. In 1947 she was appointed to teach at Loscoe Road Girls School, and Miss McLening makes frequent reference to her energy and enthusiasm with regard to school trips in the log. Here are just a few -

July 13th 1948 - Mrs Cook took a party of leavers to the pottery this afternoon. October 6th 1948 - Mrs Cook and Miss White took seniors on a tour of Derbyshire visiting Eyam, Castleton and caves, Ladybower and Hathersage. November 4th 1948, Mrs Cook took a party of 20 of her class to Dale Abbey in connection with their study of Derbyshire this afternoon. July 1949, Junior 4 were taken by Mrs Buxcey and Mrs Cook to Chatsworth this afternoon. June 20th 1957, Mrs Cook and Miss Watson took Junior 4 to Thoresby Hall this afternoon.

In the 1930's and 40's Mrs Cook had her own car and was one of the few women drivers in those days. Mr Barry Cook told me that she once parked on Wilmot Street at the Market Place, forgot to put the car in gear and worse - with no break on!

"It had rolled down the slope a little way. When she came out of the Co-op and saw a big man pushing her car back up the hill - she went white with horror!"

*"Is this **your** car Mrs?"*

Mrs Cook retired from William Howitt Secondary Modern School in July 1962. She was to enjoy a further 18 years with her husband. Mr Percy Ward Cook died at the Derwent Hospital Derby in 1980 at the age of 84. The old lady suffered a stroke in October 1986 shortly after a holiday in Skegness. It became necessary for her to move into the Orchard Nursing Home. On September 19th 1990, at the age of 87, the minutes of a fondly remembered and totally committed teacher - finally ran out.

On my re-visit to the Howitt campus, I approached in the same way as I had done as a pupil, from the foot of High Street up Allandale Road. Into the pleasant leafy surroundings, past the old green canteen on the right and on up to a hallowed spot where Mrs Cook's prefabricated glassy classroom stood on the left. An emotional moment as I silently stood and reverently looked at the site of the happiest year of my life. Not the original wooden building of forty years ago, but one of a more modern construction in exactly the same place. It was about half an hour after school and three young teachers were sitting within, chatting, laughing and relaxing after a stressful and hard working day. I resented them! I wanted to tell them to get out of Mrs Cook's room! In that place, at that time, their frivolous conduct was somehow disrespectful. A totally illogical reaction as this was now their territory and **I** was the intruder. This class was for me a shrine. It was all that was left of Mrs Cook. I felt the need to pay homage, to grieve for the Lady and the long lost time.

After explanations the present staff kindly welcomed me into my old room and one woman could remember what she described as

"..a rotting old shed ...was rebuilt in 1989. Many teachers
will have worked in here over the last forty years."

I sat in the place where I used to sit, and looked around at the approximate places of my friends - and then at Her desk. Indulging in a brief dramatic reconstruction of the jolly times, I was reminded of a line from Dickens when the Ghost of Christmas Past told Scrooge -

"These are but the shadows of things which have been.
They cannot see us. They do not know we are here."

Eventually I thanked the members of staff, said 'goodbye' - and a solemn and silent 'goodbye' to the Lady who had made it possible for me to become a teacher.

Buxcey's Behaviour Camp

It would have been in the autumn of 1958 that the 'disrespectful duo' first noticed an intriguing scene in the playground after assembly when lessons were about to commence. A file of pupils in a perfectly straight line were being closely inspected by a short, slightly stout, hard faced woman with little square spectacles. "TURN" was sharply barked out and each 'soldier' obediently instantly responded . "FORWARD". The line proceeded in military step. Sensibly she remained at the rear for a clear view of her troops who were marching to one of the prefabricated classrooms near Holmes Street. "THERE'S TALK!" We could not hear anything from the second year automatons, who would not have dared to turn their heads to make eye contact, but obviously **She** did.

For Malcolm and the author, this was
the beginning of the 'Buxcey Legend'.

Of all the staff, she was the most fascinating and gave us years of endless pleasure inventing and developing comic situations based on our memories of this fierce grim and squat disciplinarian. The title of this chapter was Malcolm's immediate utterance on his observation. To the best of my memory she was not disliked. No one dreaded her classes. On the contrary, she was a rock of stability, a link with all the positive aspects of the Victorian Age.

As is often the case with inquisitive pupils, we tried to tempt Mrs Cook into making unprofessional comments on this curious compact little power house.

"Miss, isn't Mrs Buxcey strict! Don't you think so Miss?
What do you think Miss?"

Correctly, she would not be drawn beyond a simple and safe -

"Yes, she's very strict".

Seven years later at Hardy Barn, naughty Narvel again pressed his questions on the subject of the mysterious matriarch, and **this** time Mrs Cook had plenty to say as we will see later.

Back in the classroom some of the girls were glad to comment. Brenda Mac Kay did not like Mrs Buxcey. *"She has favourites!"* Carol

Oakes said - *"Oh no, she's lovely. She's really nice"*. Brenda countered this by saying that Carol had proved her point. Mrs Cook listened to all this with a half smile and ignored all further attempts to extract information.

Mrs Buxcey forcefully came to our attention during one memorable assembly. With Miss McLening firmly in charge on the stage, Mrs Mitchell playing the piano, the whole school was in full flow with 'Onward Christian Soldiers'. Above all this - suddenly, a shrieking gravely furious wail - *"Ronald Stanley - GET OUT!!"*
Silence! Everything stopped! Momentarily Mrs Mitchell's fingers hovered uncertainly in the air. All eyes turned to the red faced enraged mistress, who was now barging into the humanity of her compacted class to lay hands on her victim. To say that she actually dragged him out of the hall would be an exaggeration, but Ron was under very close arrest as Miss McLening said *"Take him to my room Mrs Buxcey"*. The latter replied with a bad tempered grunt, as her small square form disappeared through the door with its prey. The headteacher's smooth cultured tones always seem to say Mrs 'Baxcey'. With the usual Derbyshire closed 'U', everyone else pronounced it - 'Bookcey'.

For forty years I have wondered what Ron was doing to cause his little form teacher to publicly explode and disrupt the assembly. I imagined some grievous sin along erotic lines! After putting the question I was anxious for the long awaited reply -
"I can remember the incident, but can't remember what I was doing!"
He went on to tell me about his first meeting in September 1958 with the formidable dame.
"Right from day one - we didn't hit it off. I'd been on holiday at Skegness and started school a fortnight late. After a few minutes upstairs with Miss McLening, a prefect took me to Mrs Buxcey's room. She didn't like what she saw."
Ron Stanley, being a fan, looked and dressed like the popular singer Joe Brown. They were both blond and had the same short hair style. Turning up two weeks late in sexy skin tight black jeans, and closely cropped crew cut, antagonised the traditional schoolmarm. The 63 year old stood glowering at her trendy rebellious new pupil. Being born in the reign of Queen Victoria is consistent with Victorian values of moral

propriety. Like the author, Ron was put into the lowest ability group of his year, although arriving late he had never been tested.

Stormy scenes followed. A short attention span often caused the strict instructress to point a menacing bony old finger at her continually distracting golden scamp. This would be ignored resulting in an incensed bark -

*"Ronald Stanley - can't you see! I'm **POINTING** at you!!*

To be fair, Ron could <u>not</u> see. She had a bent arthritic finger of uncertain indication.

One riotous breaktime saw herds of terrified screaming shrieking girls being rounded up like frightened sheep. They were being driven on by one single fair haired boy, with something very unpleasant and slimy in his mischievous hand. The infamous Stanley had found, to his delight, a large succulent slug. The glistening repellent horror was held aloft for all the fleeing females to see, as swathes more were collected into an ever larger heaving squealing mob. This cacophony eventually brought out members of staff. I have a memory of Mrs Cook ploughing into the multitude of thrilled and excited boys in search of Ronald and his new unpopular viscous pet. It was the biggest slug we had ever seen. Perhaps the great granddaddy of the unwanted creeping mucous morsels on Malcolm's dinner plate!

Like many fit energetic and non-academic lads, the 'bane of Buxcey' excelled in sport and athletics. Good soccer skills earned him a place in the school team, in fact Ron was playing regularly up to the age of 42. In addition he became the champion intermediate cross country runner. Bad behaviour got him banned from the William Howitt Secondary Modern School football and running teams, but he was <u>so</u> good at the latter that one day the school had great and urgent need of him.

"Mr Brentnall walked into Mrs Buxcey's room with a bundle of pumps and shorts tucked under his arm. 'Come with me Stanley'. He tried to persuade me to help Howitt. 'Will you run with the seniors today?'"

Ron was angry because he had not been allowed to previously represent the school and show the world what he could achieve. Accordingly he said - "*No*".

Two generations later all is forgiven. In spite of all the aggravation he recalls Mrs Buxcey with respect and affection -

William Howitt Secondary Modern School Football Team
League Champions 1960 - 61

Mr Maurice Brentnall is standing on the left. *Top Row* - Stuart Turner, Billy Havercroft, Maurice Parkin, Graham Saxton, Alvin Marsh, Clement Cartledge, Roger Marshall and Alan Turner. *Seated* - Alan Bamford, Ron Stanley, Tommy Bridge, Melvin Brough, Geoffrey Marshall, Peter Hadfield and Ken Lilly.

"No malice. Owe were a grand owd gal. It wasn't just me.
She was fair, and treated everybody the same."
After 'playing up' Mrs Buxcey, he was temporarily moved into the class
of Mrs Leonard Smith a noted disciplinarian, like her husband, who
stood for no nonsense. Ronald was in awe of her -
"She was like a figurehead."

This effective practice of removing difficult pupils is still used today.
No teaching is possible without discipline. In my comprehensive
school, having the reputation of being strict, some of my colleagues had
fallen into the habit of sending me badly behaved pupils they could not
control.
"Send them to Narvel. They're terrified of him."
This regardless of the fact that I had already been given tough classes.
Here is the irony. I was regarded as a conservative and reactionary, and
yet considered useful in holding the line against the very anarchy the
progressives have created!

Continuing problems brought Ronald Stanley into our room for a
time. It was quite natural that he should sit next to David Martin.
Younger he may have been, but Ron was a force to be reckoned with.
Like David, he was treated with respect. Alas Malcolm thought better
of it, and there were never any cartoons of the 'assembly' or 'slug'
incident. However, the 1998 Mr Stanley has been a good sport and
most co-operative in the production of this book. He became fond of
Mrs Cook, remembered her advice, found it useful all his life and
repeated it to his own lad.
"I'd say - 'I can't do this Miss'. She would reply - 'There's no
such word as 'can't'.' You can always overcome a problem."

In Mr Brentnall's form, Mrs Buxcey took history and I heard her own
version of the above when a girl said -
"I can't do this Miss." "How do you spell 'can't'."
"Err..c.a.r - ." "NO!! M-U-S-T. MUST!"
Ron went on to express the views shared by many of our generation
with regard to courtesy and consideration for older people.
"I think back to what those teachers told us. They were right.
We may have had our fun, but unlike some of
today's kids we always respected our elders."

Ronald Stanley and his Mates
From left to up and over - Geoffrey Marshall, Ron Stanley, Peter Stimpson and Terry Warner. *In the background behind Terry* - Maurice Parkin. *In front* - Glen Jenkins

I came to respect Carol Bestwick after she gave me a massive great thump I thoroughly deserved! My only experience of physical violence at William Howitt Secondary Modern School. Carol was a big girl and one of our number made a humorous comment at her expense. A comment I thought it fun to repeat to her. She was <u>not</u> amused as I quickly discovered. Having introduced Carol, I can now proceed to the most fraught part of Mrs Buxcey's lesson - the beginning. Often the most fraught part of any lesson, rather like the 'take off' in an aircraft. Once you are up and going - it gets easier. After standing in a straight silent line outside, we were commanded to enter, as she stood sentry like a grim squat granite monolith. Fascinated by this woman, I watched her face as we filed by and took our seats. The expression, although mostly stern, had interesting variations depending upon who was passing. Generally the harsh countenance was relaxed to neutrality for girls, but firmed up to an unforgiving hardness for boys. After all, she had spent most of her professional life teaching single sex classes, and the recent challenge of co-education must have been unwelcome so near to the end of her career. Occasionally a passing girl would acknowledge her mistress with a polite smile and Mrs Buxcey would, just for an instant, soften her features to one of her rare beams - until the next boy passed. Periodically this ritual was interrupted by - 'incidents'.

Here I must empathise and feel deep sympathy for this strict lady. Like the author some four decades on, she was trying to maintain the high standards of the past, during a period of permissive change. Had she lived, Mrs Buxcey would have witnessed the 'Swinging Sixties', mini skirts, Carnaby Street, hippies, the obscene lyrics of the musical 'Hair', 'flower power' and find out 'where it's at'! A lot for an intolerant conservative old lady. Like the traditional 'miserable old Mr Annable' of the 1990's, she was fighting a loosing battle holding back the flood.

'Incidents'! Small things which had to be dealt with, but would cause much stress and put many miles on the human clock. I do not remember what Carol Bestwick did to irk the woman. Not much by modern standards. Perhaps she talked, or was distracted in some minor way, but enough to warrant a sharp reprimand. Carol felt she had been 'shouted at' unjustly and registered her objection in the only unspoken way she could. A furious deep red faced glower was shot at the squat square schoolmarm. It must have had about the same level of impact as Carol's fist had on me! Feeling the impact of these 'daggers', the indignant Buxcey drew herself up to her full five foot three inches and said - *"And I am the one who should be annoyed - NOT you."*
Thirty five years later, a rude unruly girl did **much** more to earn a 'telling off' from the author, and responded with a similar 'evil eye'. Without thinking I spoke the exact same words as the buxom dame -
"And I am the one who should be annoyed - NOT you."
At the instant the words had left my mouth, I remembered Howitt, Carol Bestwick, and thought -
*"Oh no! My God! I'm turning into **Mrs Buxcey!!**"*

Another 'coming into the classroom' incident involved Graham Waterall and his friend Michael Annable. It has to be said that the conduct of both lads rarely fell short of excellent, but on this occasion they managed to inflame our history ma'am who ordered them to stand at the front where they endured the sharp edge of her tongue. The drama

153

and tension of the situation, together with a grinning facing audience brought on a fit of the giggles. This had an incendiary effect on the already burning Buxcey, now protesting in a higher pitch. No use! The original titters which they had desperately repressed, had now developed into disobedient open shaking convulsions. Experience has taught me to 'go with the flow' when the giggles arrive. Short of standing over the chuckling culprits with a raised axe, very little can be done.

The humour of the next incident is based on a difference between the open honest unsuspecting nature of the fourteen year old Derek Goostrey, and the sixty four year old worldly sarcastic biting Buxcey. She, of frosty features was watchfully policing a deep silence, save for the faint movement of pens. Suddenly this industrious peace was broken by the voice of authority - *"Derek Goostrey!"*
All eyes turned to the innocent Derek who had been beavering away over his book. In anxiety, his youthful fresh face coloured and looked up for further instructions. *"Come Out! Bring your book."*
After the style of impending execution, up plodded Derek, reverently placing his exercise book before the searching matriarchal square spectacles. What followed next took us all by surprise. Her hard voice and features softened to a faint shadow of a smile.
"It's nice writing isn't it?"
Instant relief showed on the pleasant round countenance of the unaffected credulous Goostrey, so typical of both twin brothers.
"Yes, it is very nice writing."
The naive lad could not believe his luck and risked a smile.
"You must be proud of this writing!"
Derek Goostrey positively beamed and nodded in enthusiastic agreement - until, to his horror, the despotic dame had quickly resumed her more natural tyrannical glare and gravely curdling threatening voice.
"It is a mess! **Disgraceful!** *Do it again!!"*

Much as I admire the traditional side of Mrs Buxcey with her firm hold on discipline, as one historian to another, a reluctant note of criticism becomes necessary. I have no memory of a single time that she ever addressed the class and introduced, or explained a topic of history. To the best of recollection it was an instruction to read the chapter and write about it. The modern OFSTED inspectorate would take a disparaging view of such simple uninspiring lesson plans. But here was
154

a lady approaching 65 at the very end of a long career, and as we will see later, her imaginative energy was well documented in the past.

It is ironic that Mrs Buxcey would have found my classes much too noisy and trivial, and yet my progressive colleagues did not like what they saw as long stretches of sterile silences in Room 78. Hours were spent producing worksheets which were seen as too factual and competitive. The noise and competition came from my 'Class Quiz' which was used to warm up the start of each lesson as a review of the previous lesson. Cards bearing the name of each pupil were arranged on my desk face down. A question was asked **before** a card was turned and named. All were on their toes, since nobody knew when they would become accountable to explain a part of the subject they **should** know. Eventually every name in the class would be called. To add an element of spice, the pupils beforehand agreed to suffer a minor penalty imposed for a wrong answer - usually to stand up. I think Mrs Buxcey would approve of **that** part! The unanswered question would be offered for an extra point, and a winner declared at the end of the quiz. The silence came from my worksheets of very short questions requiring even shorter written answers. Each unit of work was regularly tested with multiple choice or 'mix 'n match' papers under examination conditions. Historical information and understanding was being measured in the most quick, concise and efficient way.

Perhaps it is unfair to make an unfavourable comparison between the Buxcey and Annable classroom practice, which after all are separated by a half century of educational development. If my lessons were more animate and colourful, it is due to imaginative textbooks, videos, computers and double teacher training.

Mrs Doris Cook told me that Mrs Buxcey never went to college at all. As we will see below, she did very well with her sound secondary education and a two year teaching practice which is the most valuable and effective component of any teacher training. I am not in any position to comment on the quality of university teacher training in the early years of this century. However I can confidently tell the reader, from first hand experience, that colleges of education since the 1960's, in this country and in the United States, have been dominated by left wing progressive lecturers and professors. Their egalitarian philosophy has done much more to damage generations of children than Mrs Buxcey's lack of a formal teaching certificate.

Joyce Clay has affectionate memories of a younger Mrs Buxcey in the late 1940's.

"She was the matronly type. Strict, but nice with it."

Miss Beryl Briggs and her friend Miss Mary McLening both liked Mrs Buxcey.

"You could always turn to her for help. She was small
and compact, reminding me of my grandmother."

As staff they were always on formal terms with each other, Miss Briggs did not know her Christian name and finding it was difficult, until ex-pupil Kath Syson nee Wilbur, rang me one morning and said -

"I'm going to sing to you! Be ready to fill the gap.
'Come into the garden......'"

On stressful days at the comprehensive school, some of my wiser fellow teachers warned me that I had only so many tantrums left to throw, and each one would shorten my life. This reminded me of Mrs Buxcey's short retirement. Miss McLening marked the occasion with a brief announcement in July 1960.

"Mrs Buxcey is leaving us at the end of term. I know that Mrs Buxcey made you work, but I am sure you will all join me in wishing her a well earned happy and long retirement."

She went to live in Ayrshire, and was once visited by her former headteacher and Miss Briggs when they were touring in Scotland. I was intrigued that the latter had no clear memory of <u>Mr</u> Buxcey, so dominant was his redoubtable spouse. A regular attender to the lectures of the Heanor and District Local History Society, it would seem her main interest was history. Beyond this, it had been very difficult to find any information about Maud Buxcey. Miss Briggs suggested this was because -   *"She kept herself to herself, and tended to speak*
to equals who shared her historical interests."

All ex-pupils seemed to know one main fact about the little authoritarian schoolmarm -

"Mrs Buxcey! Oh yes, she lived round the
corner from the school on Park Street."

156

Derek Goostrey who lived round the next corner, told me that if she was spotted in time, the local kids and pupils would clear off out of her way! In this I envied Mrs Buxcey!

A strict well respected school teacher who could walk the streets of Heanor without any fear whatsoever. How very different from today when I know to my cost that a strict traditional teacher who makes pupils work in silence is subject to frequent verbal assaults in public.

At the interview of my comprehensive school, the headmaster gave me good advice -

"Make sure that you live at least five miles from the school."

One respected, firm and stern Head of Year lived 'round the corner' from the school for many years without any problems until the progressives loosened the ties of control and punishment. After that his life became a nightly hell when his house was regularly beset by yobs and slags chanting obscenities who had little to fear **even** if they were successfully identified. Nearly four years after retirement, I would still feel very uncomfortable walking through the centre of a certain North Midland town.

It is against this sorry background that I look back fondly to the days of Mrs Buxcey and even further back to the distant days of Mr Billy Smith. Barry Forster told me that in the early 1940's -

"If we chanced to meet a master on the streets after
school, we had to salute and say - 'Good evening Sir'".

I had thought that this chapter would end here. This little mysterious lady had taken her carefully guarded privacy to the grave. Even the multitude of Radio Derby listeners could shed no further light on the intriguing woman behind the iron mask she wore during nearly half a century of teaching. Until one day I spoke to John Wright. He put me in touch with a man who was a full ocean and a continent away in Victoria, British Columbia, Canada.

He was another 'Stanley', but this was Stanley **Buxcey!**

I am most grateful to Mr Buxcey for enabling me to tell the full story of Heanor's most celebrated and formidable dame.

We must go back 103 years in time, but only a few miles to the sleepy little village of Smalley. On August 20th 1895 in the reign of Queen Victoria, Sarah Ann Earnshaw was delivered of a daughter - Maud. She was to be the only child of Sarah and Robert Earnshaw who was a framework knitter.

157

The Early Days of Maud Earnshaw

Top left - A 1907 photograph of Miss Maud Earnshaw with her father Robert and mother Sarah Anne, *Top right* - Very early photograph of young Maud, about 1902. *Bottom* - About 1910, a chemistry class at Blyth Secondary School. The well behaved studious looking Maud is the centre girl on the second row.

UNIVERSITY OF OXFORD.

Maud Earnshaw ————————————————

born the *20th* day of *August* in the year 1895 ,

passed the OXFORD LOCAL EXAMINATION as a Senior Candidate in the year 1912 ,

at the *Newcastle-upon-Tyne* Centre, under the Index Number 37 ,

and is hereby declared an

ASSOCIATE IN ARTS OF THE UNIVERSITY OF OXFORD.

——————————————
Vice-Chancellor.

Subjects in which the Candidate satisfied the Examiners.

—— *Arithmetic; Religious Knowledge;* ——
—— *History;* ——
—— *English Language & Literature including Composition;* ——
—— *Geography.* ——

The Candidate was placed in the Pass List.

SECRETARY TO THE DELEGACY.

At some point in the early 1900's the family moved to the coastal resort of Blyth in Northumberland. Young Maud must have found her new home agreeable with its three miles of white sandy beach in front of wooded parkland stretches. At 14 she attended Blyth Secondary School in 1909 until 1912 when she went to Newcastle on Tyne, and successfully sat the Associate in Arts Examination of the University of Oxford. This must have been the Edwardian equivalent of 'A' Levels. For the next two years up to the age of 19 she was a pupil teacher at Plessey Road Council School in Blyth, and the headteacher predicted that with further experience, she would become an intelligent and

159

useful teacher. That concluded the formal training. In 1914 the Earnshaws moved back to Heanor. To be close to her parents, Maud took up her first teaching post at Sheffield. Mr John Hope's writing is not legible enough to discern the name of the school, (I'm sure Derek Goostrey's writing is much better) but he also tactfully refers to her lack of experience. Clearly we have yet some way to go before this attractive young lady will fully develop into the powerful force forever branded into the educational souls of future Heanorians!

In April 1916 young Maud joins the staff of Loscoe Road School where she will be teaching for the next 44 years. On the precious old photograph in Chapter 4 she stands on the left, as a very junior member of staff, humbly posed, obediently and neatly with hands behind the back. The only other person we can positively identify is the seated headmaster in the centre, the founder of Mundy Street Boys School - the all powerful confident autocrat - Mr Henry Dix. As with all photographs in this book, please contact me if you can identify the un-named.

I was entranced by these ancient photographs of the once pretty young mistress, and looked hard for some small resemblance to the old lady I well remember. A slightly square face and hint of seriousness were the only slender comparisons. The cruel years had taken their terrible toll, as is the case for us all in the fullness of time. A wave of affection and remorse swept over me for all the exploitation of the remarkable amusing character. But youth will always poke fun at the older generation, as was the crusty old strict Mr Annable, a suitable target for <u>his</u> pupils.

After three and a half years we get a Loscoe Road School testimonial from Mr Jackson who makes the very first reference to Miss Earnshaw's later formidable reputation -
> *"She is a capable disciplinarian and she is able to obtain*
> *the best from her class with the minimum of effort."*

Maud eventually met a man called Adam, and in 1924 at the age of 29 she married him. After the ceremony she emerged with the name which for generations of Loscoe Roaders will always be synonymous with discipline, obedience, behaviour and silent hard work.

She was now the fully fledged, the one and only - **Mrs Buxcey!**

160

Loscoe Road School Staff about 1921

Seated centre is the headmaster Mr Charles Mettam. On the extreme right, standing is Miss Maud Earnshaw. If you can identify any of the other teachers, please let me know.

In a valuable long and informative letter, Mr Stanley Buxcey (by diplomatic understatement) has revealed a great deal about his mother which appears to be parallel to the experience of Mr Barry Cook. Like Mrs Doris Cook, her friend and colleague Mrs Maud Buxcey was first and foremost - a thoroughly dedicated professional teacher.

And didn't we know it!

"Her marriage was not entirely subservient to her professional interests and family life was at least as pleasant as was reasonable at that time. My father Adam Joseph Buxcey was a joiner by trade. He was the eldest child of Edwin Joseph Buxcey a builder who had taken his son out of school at the age of 13 (1907) to serve as a general help in the builder's yard. My father was not unintelligent, but the differences in educational experience and attitudes were something of a problem."

In the 1920's and 1930's the Loscoe Road School log frequently refers to the comings and goings of Mrs Maud Buxcey who was almost continually present as a supply teacher. This hard work and extra income gave them a higher living standard which included the running of an Austin Seven. Young Stanley remembers -

"Saturday shopping trips to Derby, Sunday afternoon picnics in the Peak District and summer trips to the east coast, generally Skegness."

But Maud the mother became the unrelenting familiar Mrs Buxcey we all know when Stanley started school -

*"My mother's educational philosophy was **rigorously** applied to her son who was given supplementary work at home, especially in arithmetic prior to taking the scholarship examinations for Heanor Secondary (Grammar) School, successfully. When my class standing fell, my pocket money was reduced! When my class standing had been restored to an acceptable level - so was my pocket money."*

Such it was to be a child of Mrs Buxcey.

The British economy improved after 1935 and the Buxceys started to take summer holidays and Christmas breaks at Bournemouth and Torquay. The teenage Stanley was encouraged to play tennis by his mother, who also enjoyed the game. Adam Buxcey was absorbed by his ornamental and vegetable gardening. In March 1940, grandfather Edwin J Buxcey died. Adam moved to take over his late father's builders yard at the well known address of 9 Park Street, where they

162

lived for the next 20 years. Mrs Maud Buxcey returned to full time teaching.

Mother's academic pressure paid off because Stanley Buxcey went up to Manchester University in 1942 and he followed in her footsteps. The Loscoe Road School log entry of September 22nd 1950 -

> *"Mr Stanley Buxcey completed a period (10 days)*
> *of observation and teaching practice."*

In 1951 he was appointed to a position at the Henry Mellish Grammar School in Bulwell. 1954 saw him married and the following year he moved to teach in Canada. Mrs Buxcey must have been very proud of her successful son.

During the war years the Buxceys became active in old time dancing at the Heanor Town Hall with a small group of Loscoe Road School teachers. Later they achieved the level of 'Gold Bar Certificate' at Blackpool in 1948 and went on to Scottish Country Dancing at Dunoon.

Apart from shaking with rage, I find it difficult to picture a dancing Mrs Buxcey, but the documentary evidence is conclusive.

So the popular conception of the old Victorian narrow disapproving strict squat grumpy historian, is now shattered; and the lady is revealed to have a surprising and colourful range of interests, hobbies and talents.

But back at school it is business as usual.

In 1929 Mr Mettam wrote in his heavy hand - *"She is an excellent teacher and a capital disciplinarian."* In 1931, Winifred A Westland refers to Mrs Maud Buxcey's - *"..strong powers of discipline, she proved herself a very valuable and efficient help."*

There follows a set of documents which chart key stages in Mrs Buxcey's career.

PLESSEY ROAD COUNCIL SCHOOL,

BLYTH,

May 26th 1914

—— Miss Maud Earnshaw has served her Pupil Teachership in this school, and has shown herself to be capable, with further experience and effort, of becoming an intelligent and useful teacher. —

She is punctual, regular in attendance, and in general has given satisfaction in the performance of her duties.

Ag. Forster
Head Teacher

164

JOSEPH L. GIBBONS, F.C.S.,
Head Master.

28. X. 14

Miss Maud Earnshaw was a student here for over three years, & I am pleased to state that during the whole of that time her conduct and work gave me every satisfaction.

She is earnest, intelligent, conscientious and most industrious: she will, I believe, prove most helpful in carrying on the work of an elementary school, — and I have therefore pleasure & confidence in recommending her.

(Signed) J. L. Gibbons

Derbyshire Education Committee.

Loscoe C of E Boys' School.

Heanor 25/6/ 29 192

Mrs Buxcey was a member of
the Staff of this school for about
8 years during the whole of
that time filling loyally wholly-
heartedly into her duties
& loyally served the school
& interests of the school.
She is an excellent teacher
& a capital disciplinarian
& always obtained the best
of manners with the class
Placed under her charge, to
it was a decided loss to
this school, when through
marriage, she was obliged
to sever her connections
with it.

The duty is too arduous, &
no time too long if she
can serve the welfare of the
children.

She has for the last
fortnight been on supply
work at this school, Keen
managing the same, Keen
spared for work; & loyally
co-operated with the rest
of the staff in all the
activities of the school
both in & out of school
hours.

I can safely recommend
her for any duties in school,
Knowing, valuing her
capabilities worth

Chas. Bratten
Head Master

Derbyshire Education Committee.

Heanor. Loscoe Rd. C. Girls School.

12^d Jan. 1924.

Mrs Buxcey commenced as
uncertificated supply teacher in the
High Street Temporary School on the
1st Feb. 1926 and has proved a
very real help there.

She is a capable teacher,
especially of junior children,
industrious and conscientious, and
she employs good methods. She
has the welfare of the children at
heart, she surmounts difficulties
and her teaching generally is most
successful.

Winifred A. Westland.
Head Mistress.

167

DERBYSHIRE LOCAL EDUCATION AUTHORITY

SOUTH-EAST DIVISIONAL EXECUTIVE

P. J. T. GRANT, M.A.
Divisional Education Officer

Our Reference JP/299/15/MH

Telephone :
ILKESTON 924

Your Reference

EDUCATION OFFICE,
1, HEANOR ROAD,
ILKESTON.

19th May, 1960.

Dear Mrs. Buxcey,

Heanor Howitt Secondary School

The Divisional Executive at their last meeting received notice of your resignation from the staff of the above named school, and on their behalf I was asked to thank you for your long and valuable services to the Authority and wish you a very happy retirement.

Yours sincerely,

[signature]

Mrs. M. Buxcey,
9, Park Street,
Heanor,
Derbyshire.

168

In the 1940's John Wright, who was at Loscoe Road Boys School recalls the firm schoolmarm teaching his class old folk songs -
"Beating the time with a stick as she came down between us. If you didn't sing the right note, she whacked you across the back of the shoulders!"
Is it possible that Mrs Buxcey ever met Miss Madge Calder?
Mr Wright did not think that the lads in his class would look back on the strict Mrs Buxcey with much affection, but -
"We were an unruly lot and needed discipline. She was not averse to giving you four strokes of the cane. Oh my word yes!!

The 1950's brought little joy to Maud Buxcey who had to struggle with increasing personal problems at home. Mr Adam Buxcey refused to have a much needed hip replacement and -
"My mother had to cope with his increasing disability and irascibility for the remainder of her life. She also had to look after her own mother who lived on her own in deteriorating health until her death in November 1959."
After forty years, this explains a puzzling and very rare moment, when Mrs Buxcey, in unusual soft tones, once apologised for mislaying a record of awarded house points -
"I'm not quite myself today having had some bad news."
Characteristically, she did not elaborate, but we were all touched and deeply sorry.

Mrs Buxcey the carer continued to minister to the needs of Mr Buxcey the invalid who ended up surviving her by 18 years!

Stan Buxcey (as he signed himself) said that in 1960 -
"After a life of consistent effort, my mother was finally able to retire at the age of 65."
Maud and Adam moved 250 miles north of Heanor all the way up to Mauchline, Ayrshire, west of the Scottish Lowlands, ten miles from the Firth of Clyde. In this farming town, noted for making curling stones and its associations with Robert Burns; the Buxceys settled into Redgate Cottage. A large garden had been chosen for Adam, but according to his son -
"It was too far north and they found the short winter days and long cold nights dreadful. By November 1962 they had made the decision to move south to Bournemouth."

They had also planned to visit him in California the following year. Mr Stanley Buxcey has kindly sent me a copy of the very last letter he received from his mother written on November 9th 1962. A touching letter in a neat clear hand speaking of the simple every day chores such as washing dishes and clearing away while 'the pater' is reading. She speaks of shopping, the onset of winter and wet weather. The tone of this letter is gentle kind and loving. Finally we now see behind the dedicated professional mask into the heart of this genial, conscientious, considerate and affectionate lady.

In the days which followed, the stressful hard years took their toll. She complained of ominous pains in the shoulder. On the afternoon of November 17th she went into the kitchen to prepare tea. It took a long time. Too long. Mr Buxcey found her dead on the floor.

Maud Buxcey was a character worthy of Dickens. A living link with the Victorian period when children were expected to be 'seen and not heard'. We will not see her like again. All those who knew Mrs Buxcey would wish to associate themselves with the generous and affectionate tribute paid to her by Ronald Stanley in the Horsley Woodhouse vernacular -
"Owe were a grand owd gal!!"

Quoting Horace

My years at Mundy Street Boys School gave me a healthy respect and interest in the school power chain. I am not sure when I first noticed what became a familiar group of big lads, who regularly strode through the Howitt playground with an air of authority. Their leader was a distinctively dazzlingly blond, flashing his good looks to admiring girls, some of whom were trying to pretend a lack of interest. In complete confidence, he swaggered a well proportioned athletic body in the midst of a strutting Mafia of disciples. At some variance to the lean strapping image, this fair-haired youth had a keen quick sense of humour. Risqué but clever one liners were delivered to bystanders in a deep sexy voice to the delight of all. Even the teachers had to laugh at the flirtatious banter of this flaxen embryonic comedian. He could carry it - **we** would have been in trouble. We took great care to laugh with him - never **at** him.

Forty years later, Horace Hart had some difficulty recognising the

young man described above, but in that same sensuous seductive voice which has never deserted him, he said -

"I saw myself more as a gentle giant. I never hit anybody, nor had so much kudos! I wouldn't rate myself with the likes of Terry Hutchinson, Terry Grace, Pete Lambert or David Martin."

His modesty was as much then as it is today. The dashing young Horace was never arrogant or a braggart. His quips were never cruel. He never had to prove anything.

He was simply, Horace - the King of the School.

Terry Miles with a slightly
younger Horace.

Many aspects were admirable, but the prestige came chiefly from his prowess on the sports field. At the high jump, he beat everybody and went on to represent the school at Cotmanhay. The starting level was so low, he asked them to raise it to save time! Eventually he cleared 5ft. 2", one inch over the district record. The school hero was thrilled -

"Another inch and I'll be able to leap over Mrs Buxcey!"

A pity Malcolm had left the previous July. I imagined a cartoon showing a butch hunky Horace just clearing our angry faced history mistress with one giant jump!

Regional trials were to be held in Skegness. We were all excited when it became known that Horace was to be personally chauffeured there in Mr Brentnall's highly polished coach built Morris, with the impressive wooden dash board! Working class families did not own cars and few of us ever rode in one. For the honour of the school and a pupil's future, the Deputy Head was prepared to use his own vehicle and give up free time. Unfortunately the athlete was never able to compete because his father refused the required permission.

"Horace will go to Skegness when he goes with me on holiday."

A great disappointment to all of us who were hoping for fame and fortune to descend on our popular 'Jack the Lad'.

Notwithstanding other challenges awaited, and Horace Hart was a good all round sportsman. An impressive long jumper and he did well in cross country running. The latter was encouraged at Howitt by the fitness, skills and stamina of Mr Jim Ferraby who taught woodwork and games. He had been a surveyor in the Royal Artillery stationed at Hong Kong and was a much admired role model. On the four mile route which passed Codnor Castle, he would 'run the column', dropping back to encourage and bring up the stragglers (which included the author) and spurt on to speed up the vanguard! Nearly twenty years our senior, yet he could out run us all. No exercise has ever so completely heated, exhilarated and exhausted me as cross country running. Years later I now find out that occasionally some of my fellow runners took short cuts! Malcolm tells me that the wayward Terry Miles beguiled him to run over a certain slag tip pit hill, cutting a mile off the total distance.

> *"We then hid and rested in the hedge bottom, waited for*
> *the others and tagged in behind coasting home!"*

Even Horace admits to short cuts.

> *"At the right time we jumped out of the hedge and re-joined*
> *the other runners puffing and panting out of breath."*

Terry Sullivan always completed the full circuit and was one of our best runners representing Howitt against other Derbyshire schools. He recalls being provided with proper running shoes for his daily practice. Howitt beat Codnor, and did well in the Heanor and Ilkeston regionals. One of the Codnor team was Phil Waller who went on to play for Derby County.

It was delightful to hear that same distinctive speech characteristic which Terry had back in Mrs Cook's class -

> *"When we ran against the other Derbyshire*
> *schools, we did dent come too clever!"*

Howitt was fortunate to have Terry who was also an accomplished footballer on the school team.

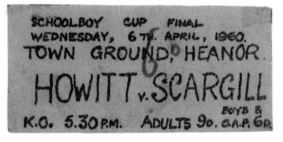

Loscoe Road School footballers were disadvantaged by the appalling ground near the Sir John Warren public house. Horace recalls -

"Dribbling round cow pats, humps and hollows, and scrabbling in the railway embankment to get the ball!"

Howittians will recall the much better ground, further on the right near the Loscoe Road Miners Welfare. Horace paid tribute to the schools skilful soccer players -

"Glyn Parker could really belt a ball. A couple of feet off the ground and as straight as a die. Alan Bamford was like Stanley Matthews, a brilliant footballer."

Horace did not mention Malcolm, who was nevertheless proud of his brand new 'Stanley Matthews' football boots when he first played at Howitt, all confident and rearing to go having been picked as the centre half. Until -

"I had the ball, but to my horror, bearing down on me at great speed - the massive unstoppable roaring red faced powerful David Martin!!
Wisely Malcolm put life and limb before possession of the ball - and fled!

In the summer of 1960, I rose to the challenge of many exhilarating cycling hours with Horace along the Derbyshire country lanes. He was fast. At one time, together with Pete Lambert and Terry Grace, they were keeping up with a double decker bus all the way from Smalley to Heanor.

The weekly visit to the open air Langley Baths is well remembered by all who froze and shivered there! David Martin and Horace Hart were powerful swimmers, but the first thing they looked for coming down Hands Road, was the amount of smoke floating out of the old chimney. A belching black mass ascending into the Langley skies, would **still** promise cold water, but **less** cold than if there were less smoke. Mr Brentnall once told us to stop moaning and being mardy - *"It's 68 degrees"*. I learned then that 68 degrees was **not** very warm. We continued to tremble. A far cry from the warm and hygienic indoor Belper Baths. Langley had two pools protected by high walls, one shallow and one deep. They were overhung by trees which meant plenty of leaves, beetles, flies and frogs to keep us company.
Yet we all remember happy times there, whether in school, House competitions or just plain having fun. Sadly an amusing photograph of Horace on the 'greasy pole' is lost.

The colloquialisms of this mining area are an integral part of its charm and interest. Earthy 'pit talk' is almost a separate language. It is difficult to understand the origin of 'owe', meaning 'she' or 'her'. Hence a recalled remark about a girl in fear of using a defective toilet -
"Owe dosna goo un arr lav."

174

My Uncle Wilfred arriving at Grandma's house kindly asked me not to leave on his account - *"Tha nedna goo fa may."*

Becoming ill - *"A were took bad."*

The father of a pal came into his bedroom with a morning cup of tea. My friend told me how he was horribly and painfully embarrassed by the following uncalled for observation - *"As got tent oop lad!"*

Just before going out on a date, I was tickled by a mother's criticism with regard to the state of her daughter's hair -

"Ee lass, tha looks a bogga abart t'ed!"

After living in America for thirteen years, I was fascinated by hearing once again, the almost forgotten frequently used endearment - 'duck'. The most 'ducks' in Heanor were uttered in the dear old Milk Bar near the top of High Street.

"Cuppa tea dook? Ee ar dook. Threepence dook.
Thanks dook. Ears ya change dook."

This was a popular meeting place especially for the Sixth Form of the Heanor Grammar School after four o'clock. On the hot thirsty afternoons of 1959, I called in for a glass of orange juice en route to Belper. *"Sixpence dook."* With the relatively new luxury of an ice cube, it was like nectar. The hi-tech garish juke box would often be playing ('Til) I Kissed You, sung by the Everly Brothers, over the buzz of distinctly non-erudite Grammar School conversation. Threepence for one selection or five for a shilling. Intimidated by the big butch lads, I did not hang around - in and out. Once one of them said -

"Yo get quicker youth!"

Pam Carter told me -

"I never went near the Milk Bar which
was considered to be a 'den of iniquity'."

Only the teachers actually said <u>H</u>orace. The rest of us simply said 'Oris'. Common speech may have held us back socially, but it was not a real problem until I lived in the United States. They frequently misunderstood me. I had to learn to sound the 'H', especially with the word '<u>h</u>ouse'. Eyebrows would be raised when I said -

"Are ya coomin ta ar ass?"

After the Easter Holiday of 1960, leavers had reduced the numbers in both 'A' and 'B' classes. Accordingly they were merged and I found myself in the same class as Horace Hart, twins Barry and Derek Goostrey for these last precious months of Howitt.

If the beginning of Howitt had constituted a 'sea change', Narvel Annable was now about to undergo another and even grander metamorphosis. Gradually, almost without noticing, I was more and more at the side of this British 1960 version of 'the Fonz'. The chemistry was working and evolving. The 'King' was slowly beginning to notice and even like me. He found me funny and we began to bounce lines off each other.

Eventually I became a friend of Horace Hart.

In personal terms I had finally climbed up the steep slope from the nadir of Mundy Street Boys School to the zenith of William Howitt Secondary Modern School.

Horace was amused at my impression of Tony Hancock impersonating Robert Newton's interpretation of Robert Louis Stevenson's colourful character - Long John Silver, from his 1881 book 'Treasure Island'. In fact my new friend asked for tuition. I suggested he imagine a limp broken neck, and throw the head to the other side on the line - *"Aarr Jim lad!"*. This was about the only line we knew other than - *"Avast there!"* and *"What fool cut a Bible!"* With the Goostrey's joining in, we had the others falling about in stitches. A daft quartet of one legged 'Silvers' hopping around the playground on an imaginary crutch with an invisible parrot on ye shoulder. It sounded like an old high pitched squeaking gate when I attempted -

"Pieces of Eight - squawk - Pieces of Eight - screech."

"That parrot needs oiling!" - responded Horace.

This nautical romp suddenly stopped when Mr Rigby appeared and pointed out that the bell had gone two minutes before!

For the main part Heanor folk were relatively poor, but most of us had the 'Telly'. Out of a choice of just two channels, the popular selection was Commercial Television which was now five years old. To further amuse and delight my new audience, I took to mimicking a frequent advert. A sort of 'drag act', I affected the accent and manner of a roughly spoken dowdy low class woman responding to questions about a new soap powder -

"Since av bin usin t' Omo, thes noow neeed fa me - ta use bleach!"

176

Under the protection and endorsement of my dominant friend, long suppressed dormant abilities of humour and entertainment were released, with positive effect giving me a new and unheard of confidence. In all the years since then, I have never enjoyed such a high level of sustained popularity.

To be a fully paid up member of 'Oris's select inner circle, my unusual name presented something of a problem. It was tacitly agreed that Horace could not be heard addressing his 'side kick' as 'Narvel'. He rolled it around a little - Narvel / marble? At that moment the author was re-Christened and re-invented. Dobba!

Philip Eggleshaw of the Heanor and District Local History Society recalls playing marbles in the early years of this century -
"A large heavy marble was rolled to try to knock the others out of a ring on the pavement. A boy was lucky if he owned a cast iron ball or 'dobber', about one and a half inches in diameter, cast in a local foundry."

Horace Hart gave me more than a new name. He bestowed some of his kudos, prestige and authority which made the summer of 1960 the happiest ever.

It is interesting to note that the 'comic quartet' were all born within six days of each other, Horace being the youngest, making his first appearance on July 18th 1945. Dobba the oldest on the 12th, and the Goostreys on the 16th, Barry arriving half an hour before Derek.
These were the austere grey days just after World War II. Hitler had shot himself only two months before. We, in a war torn Britain were born under a new Labour Government which had come to power with an overwhelming majority and ambitious plans for a new Welfare State. Almost in celebration of the coming of the Goostreys, on the day before, Britain was ablaze with light after nearly six years of blackout and dim-outs. On the very day of their birth, the first ever atomic bomb was exploded in the New Mexico desert by the Americans. The flash which was seen 250 miles away, cast a shadow over the lives of us all. Hiroshima was destroyed less than three weeks later.

Horace Hart was the youngest of the four, yet physically he was far and away the oldest and very popular with the girls. A case has been made for their civilising influence, but looking back Horace, in his measured easy way of speaking, took a different view -
"They've got to be a distraction! My school career took a nose dive.

177

It was a case of ' who could I go out with next?'"

At the baths my mature friend proudly drew my attention to the short space between the top of his trunks and his navel. His luxuriant pubic hair had enthusiastically extended up into public view proclaiming new manhood! To hammer the point home he commented on those not so well blest -

"D' ya know Dobba, Goostreys aven't an air between 'em!"

The Hart's garden could be seen from the old large 1874 factory of I. & R. Morley, now demolished. Heanorians tell me that the women, part of a once thousand strong work force, who produced knitwear, stockings and socks, had something of a naughty reputation. Horace's erotic fame was such that hordes of excited and titillated factory girls would rush to the windows to cast a voluptuous eye on his underwear pegged out and hanging on the washing line! No doubt exchanging lewd remarks, giggling, elbow nudging and pointing.

Mrs Buxcey would never have approved!

But here I must bring the handsome hunk down a peg, and tell you of one lady who escaped his sexy spell - Mrs Doris Cook! About half an hour after school, I had some occasion to go into her room and was surprised to see a chastened and humble Horace emerge from her small stockroom holding a tray of jars containing paints and brushes -

"Where do you want these putting Miss?"

Her face hardened before delivering a firm answer. My friend was clearly under punishment and I made a quick exit.

A small incident in the annals of time. Yet that image of a relatively tough lad, obedient and compliant, in those few moments, has come to have great meaning in the light of future experience. Even though he towered over the little old teacher, it would not have entered his head to refuse orders, be difficult, remonstrate or threaten to go home. He did not use my appearance to become silly or fool around. Having reason to impose the detention, Mrs Cook would not have hesitated because this was the 'popular mighty Horace'. In my comprehensive school, I have known these considerations to effect the way we deal with the 'Horaces' of the 1990's.

"We'd better go easy. This one could
cause us a lot of heartache and trouble."

178

As a teacher I would like to think I was like Mr Maurice Brentnall, but as retirement approached, I fear the reality was nearer a Mrs Buxcey type! If I was growing more cantankerous every day, it was due to the continual outrage of seeing obnoxious pupils laugh in the face of authority. Some of those who read "Miss Calder's Children", and knew me as a teacher, have been kind enough to take issue with the 'Wackford Squeers' harsh image painted within its pages. One ex-pupil, Simon Arnold, has asked that I quote from one of his letters to present a view from the younger generation.

"I am now beginning to see why and how your teaching methods came about, and yes I agree with you, children do have it far too easy today."
I would like to think that Simon is typical, but in my experience his high level of courtesy and consideration is more consistent with the 1950's than the 1990's.

Horace Hart always spoke to his elders with respect. I never heard him use bad language. I have no memory of anyone swearing in William Howitt Secondary Modern School in the usual or the obscene sense. In the deepest darkest corner of the school, if the 'F' word was ever uttered - I never knew about it. Perhaps this is why Howitt, situated in rough old Heanor, was such a special place. Perhaps it is something to do with the very decency, honesty and integrity of the Top Lads whose influence and power traditionally sets the tone. Heanor can be thankful and proud of Horace Hart.

Many years later I was sitting with a very different group of people. It was a casual after dinner discussion about classical literature. A cultured erudite gathering, but some were rather pompous and too pretentious. My friends had the advantage of either a private or grammar school education, and in subtle ways were trying to impress each other by venturing opinions and offering quotations from such great names as Milton, Chaucer and Shakespeare. The tone became even more obtuse and rarefied when the subject turned to Roman poets, when we had spoken extracts in artificial enunciation, from Ovid's 'Ars amatoria' and Virgil's 'Eclogues'. Playing safe, my personal contributions to this learned discourse had dwindled to zero, until a familiar name turned up. One priggish punctilious effeminate pedant spoke of the great joys and rewards of studying the Latin lyric poet Horace (65BC to 8BC). He trotted out something about "gather ye rosebuds while ye may", and then mischievously turned the group's attention to one who was once known as Dobba!

Being open about my early humble education at a secondary modern school, it was clear to all that I knew nothing of Roman poets. Accordingly there was an element of sadistic satisfaction when this particular pedant said -

"Narvel! You are very quiet! Can you quote Horace?"

I looked round at the circle of pale faces with traces of sardonic smiles playing around the thin sour anaemic lips, and suddenly remembered one happy sunny afternoon in a rowing boat at Matlock Bath, long ago in better company. *"Yes I can quote Horace."*

"Ave got energy fa you dook, but not fa this."

We were having a wonderful time deep in the heavily wooded green and dank rocky ravine. My companion was panting and struggling with his oars when we heard teasing girlie giggles from aloft. We could just about see two wenches who were giving us friendly waves through the beautiful sun glinting ferns clinging to the limestone, when Horace delivered his famous line to the delight of all.

It was not the first time we had been rowing on the slow silent mysterious green Derwent. One glorious day we cycled to a favourite leafy glade in the dear old mill town of my childhood. The Belper River Gardens is an enchanted arrangement of large mossy stones, bushes and great trees maturing since 1905, when the rich and beneficent George Herbert Strutt reclaimed an old muddy osier bed. It was a place of wild willows, once used for making baskets.

The result today is a maze of rock formations, alcoves, immaculate flower beds, shaded walks, fish ponds, islets and a fountain. We walked to the riverside landing stage, where the friendly boatman told us of the three mile boating stretch going up as far as Ambergate. He also told us it would cost us half a crown! We gave each other that hopeless sad look which comes into the eyes of boys who are wanting and not having. Horace may have been a force in Heanor, but this was Belper and Mr Boatman needed his two shillings and sixpence before unchaining one of his tempting vessels.

180

At this point my thoughts wandered up steep, to the very top heights of Belper Lane. Close to the clouds where there dwelt - Sister Cynthia, who might have it within her power to launch her brother into a boat. With such fresh hope we painfully pedalled up the incline to put our case. Generous Cynthia, with two little children, could ill afford to subsidise our pleasure, but the loan was handed over without hesitation, and sad to say not paid back for many years. As we left I clearly remember the silvery tones of the young nasal sounding Adam Faith coming from Cynthia's radio. Fragments of words complete with pizzicato strings. It was a beautiful tune which stayed dancing around my head for the whole of that day.

> *"... but I can't resist the thought of being kissed by*
> *- Someone Else's Baby...."*

Like the wind we raced down the hill back to river level, and the two friends were soon in the gentle civilised lost world of Kenneth Grahame. After the style of Rat and Mole, we drifted under the willows enjoying the mottled reflected sunshine underneath the foliage, and heard the friendly Derwent rhythmically lapping our little boat. I cannot speak for Horace who was manfully grappling with the oars, but I was fully aware of the total magic and enchantment of that summer, and fully aware that it would not, and could not last. It was all held together by Howitt. The friends and friendship, and the stage upon which to perform. Like an ugly unknown blackness, leaving day was remorselessly approaching, followed by the chill wind of autumn. Soon I would be 'unwillingly creeping' *away* from school.

Overhead, the occasional flash of white from magpies, and dank nostalgic scent of tiny starred wild garlic from the bank. I looked affectionately at the happy golden oarsman laughing and splashing - and I thought -

> *"It will never get better than this!"*

And it never did.

From Now Until Forever

In those last few precious weeks, little pressure was put upon us to do any serious school work. A great deal of practical activity was happening around the school, for the school. Horace was proud of the wooden shield he carefully crafted for his house, recalling the good join down the middle. With the help of Mr Ferraby; Graham Waterall, John Lavender and two other lads constructed a lectern for the main hall. Barry Goostrey was painting when Mr Ferraby said -
> *"Don't forget Barry, the gloss goes on the **outside**!"*

Our witty woodwork teacher had an occasion to take a class of barely half a dozen lads in a large long room. He sat down at his desk facing four of us on the front row, but Ronald Rouse and his friend decided to sit at a great distance far away on the very back row. Mr Ferraby ordered them to the front immediately and said -
> *"What a pity we can't find a longer room*
> *where you two could sit even **further** back!"*

It was during this relaxed period that I first came across Mr John Rigby who had been the form teacher for the 'B' class. A well spoken smooth suave master of wonderful quiet control. Frisky as we were at this point, he simply could not be 'played up'.

Terry Miles said - *"Ya darsent say owt to 'im!"*

Liked and greatly respected by the staff, Miss Brentnall said -
> *"He was a smashing chap. A typical RAF Officer. We were all aghast*
> *when he died so young soon afterwards leaving four children."*

Miss Beryl Briggs knew the Rigby family -
"Mr Rigby senior was the headmaster of the Catholic School in Ilkeston. John was the only one of his children not to go to the Ilkeston Grammar School. Instead he attended the Catholic Becket School in Nottingham.

On July 20th 1957, at a cheering Conservative rally in Bradford, the Prime Minister Harold Macmillan made his famous speech -

183

"Most of our people have never had it so good."

This was a reference to hire purchase and the growing prosperity among ordinary people, which three years later reached a small humble terraced house in the mining village of Stanley Common.

Stereophonic sound was a new phenomenon, and thanks to the 'never-never' we took proud delivery of our new Decca Radiogram with, not one, but **three** speakers. What excitement to watch the automatic pick-up arm swing over and drop the expensive sapphire stylus on to the edge of the vinyl 7" 45 rpm record. As the needle dropped into the lead groove, an anticipatory delicious electronic 'thud' would precede the ecstatic sounds to follow. At that time the new High Fidelity recordings had reached such a high quality, that I could hear Marty Wilde draw breath between the lines of my very first single, 'Teenager in Love'.

Karaoke is not so new. I thought 'Big Time' by Adam Faith was a particularly fitting track for the image of Horace Hart. Using an old Grundig tape recorder, I suggested he try his hand at singing along side the record in the background. The result was a creditable attempt.

"When the Big Times come, am goin' to have me some..."

There he was making love to the microphone, like all teenagers, hoping his hopes and dreaming his dreams. If he failed to achieve wider acclaim, he will always be recalled as the Star of Howitt.

I have one clear poignant memory of Barry Goostrey sitting close up to the turn table, listening and watching the disc go round and round. His wondrous wide eyes were a part of a pleasant face which seemed totally fresh and unblemished by any unkind or unworthy thoughts. And this was a face which was never to age, unlike the rest of us who knew Barry, and are now able to look back over four decades.

If my Howitt days had a secret spring of love nearby, then I suggest you look for the source at 32 Nelson Street, the simple Spartan dwelling of the Goostrey's. This modest home was diffused throughout with an ineffable quality of consideration, comradeship, caring and kindness. A cheerful atmosphere was presided over by the attractive Nora Helena Dodsley, who looked a good decade younger than her 36

Loscoe Road School Football Team 1959

Top row standing - Graham Saxton, Roy Watson, Michael Annable, Glyn Parker, Denis Aistrop, John Hickling, Barry Goostrey and Mr Maurice Brentnall. *Seated* - Melvin Brough, Michael Sims, Ken Lilly, Terry Sullivan and Alan Bamford. This book is dedicated to Barry Goostrey who died only five years later.

years. Her good looks had descended to the twin sons. This in spite of the sharp punishing comment Mr Brentnall once made to Derek, after he and a few others had been amused at the sight of a perceived unusually ugly girl, who had just walked into the classroom -

"You're no oil painting Goostrey!"

Always very welcome, always comfortable, and always being treated like one of the family, 32 Nelson Street was a great place to be. Even today, the surviving brother of buoyant and uplifting personality can still work that special magic, a remaining fragment of Howitt. The Goostrey charm which defies analysis, must have something to do with a lingering essence of the childlike innocence, once exploited by Mrs Buxcey.

A dark shadow was to fall over these happy memories of teenage boyhood delights. There were many jolly hours of a cycling trio (sometimes quartet) to and from Stanley Common. Derek once fell off and had his wounds tended by the kind lady at Holly Mount Farm. Splashing fun poling the raft on Simonfield Pond, a few fields north of my home.

Three years later we were all much more grown up. I was an ocean away in a New World, and very homesick for the old familiar world which had been left behind. Barry Goostrey had graduated from his push bike to a motorcycle, and had an accident in which, ominously, he banged his head. At about the same time he had another head injury whilst roller skating. Barry was an apprentice builder at W.M. Cattermole. Young Dave Cattermole was a member of our social circle.

At the end of the working day it was noticed that Barry had not eaten all of his sandwiches, and there were other indications that he was going off his food. He started to have odd days off work which eventually increased to a week at a time. He was getting weaker. The doctor was called in who could find nothing wrong, even suggesting at one point that Barry was 'swinging the lead'. Matters got worse, much worse. Barry became too feeble to get upstairs. Derek had to carry him which was not difficult - now weighing only four stone. His bed was moved down into the front room. A specialist diagnosed a brain tumour and an operation revealed it to be malignant. He received radium treatment. It was unsuccessful.

186

In April 1964 a letter travelled the three thousand miles between Heanor and Taylor in Michigan from an ex-girl friend called Mary Clarke. Being kindly concerned at my lack of success with the opposite sex, Barry had introduced me to Mary. There followed several happy weeks of double dating between the Empire, were we sat through Barry's beloved 'Westerns', and then on to the Heanor Miner's Welfare. Barry with his Diane, Dobba with his Mary. I can still see her smiling face over her usual glass of shandy. But this was a sad letter to tell me that Barry had died on the 21st of that month.

The old cliché 'only the good die young' comes to mind, but God had his pick, and he chose the best. At the very moment this book was conceived, I knew it had to be dedicated to the lad, who embodied all which was best and decent about Howitt and the Heanor teenage era.

The lad who will always be eighteen.

The lad who was called Barry Goostrey.

Warm leisurely Saturday nights were a celebratory feature of that 1960 summer. Heanor Market Place was buzzing with friendly teenagers whose names occur in these pages. In my group it was a case of - out of the Empire or Cosy, and straight into Santa Elliot's chip shop on Ray Street for supper. *"A brilliant chippie!"* recalls Derek Goostrey. He thinks Mr Elliot's nick name came from his white hair. The very size of this social centre for the youth culture was extraordinary. It seemed to go back forever with various counters, cosy alcoves and little rooms for chairs and tables. Right at the back, one large eating area. Tea, coffee, Ovaltine, Horlix or Bovril - and a huge amount of good will and happiness.

Finally to the last afternoon at school. We were all in the canteen, cleared to form a dance hall and echoing to the sweet sounds of the old school gramophone. The sadness of those last hours is well summed up by Valerie Billett.

"We were going different ways, leaving behind friends we had worked and played with. Leaving people we had got to know and cared about. Our lives were changing and we were moving on."

I remember it exactly. Powerless to stop the clock. Listening to the flip side of Adam Faith's first big hit 'What Do You Want', which was called 'From Now Until Forever'. A beautiful song of sensuous

187

melancholia with pizzicato strings plucking at our hearts.   A silver sound for a blue mood.

From now until forever, we'll build our love together, a love that doesn't fade with time, a love I'll know will always bind.
From now until forever, my life has one endeavour, to hear you say that you'll be kind, to feel your arms cling to mine.
We'll share the joy of giving, and life will be worth living, our love will reach the greatest heights to spend our days waiting for nights.
As the years go rolling by, I'll turn to you and sigh -
We've had a good life hand in hand, and shown the world our love can stand, each day our love is newly found, which proves that you and I are bound....
From now until forever.   From now until forever. (fading)   From now until forever.   From now until forever.......

A simple message of love, hope, companionship and the passing of a lifetime, and yet a portentous song of separation foreshadowing many paths into the unknown.

This book has been an unashamed indulgence of nostalgia, but the author is fully aware that we can never go back in the personal and social sense.   As we went our separate ways, life has tempered and changed us with nearly a half century of different experiences.   Writing this book has re-united me with many of my past school friends who have learned toleration, understanding and are now even better and more gentle people.   For the most part, Howitt and Heanor were good.

It was worth remembering.   It was worth writing about.

From a completely biased, subjective and nostalgic viewpoint, in this principal photograph of the book are arrayed the finest teachers in the world!   Look long and hard.   These are the people who taught me how to teach.   These are the people who taught me how to live.

On the following page - *Top row standing from left to right* - Mrs Winifred Molly Smith (widow of Mr Leonard Smith),   Mr Peter Crofts, Miss Anne Henshaw, Mr Alan Priestley, Mrs Nancy Carswell, Mr Jim Ferraby, Mrs Dorothy Cullen (Secretary) and Mr Keith Matthewman.
Seated - Mrs Evelyn Mitchell, Miss Freda Brentnall, Mr Maurice Brentnall (deputy head), Miss Mary McLening (headmistress), Mr John Rigby, Mrs Maud Buxcey and Mrs Doris Cook.

188

The Staff of William Howitt Secondary Modern School 1960

Headmistress:
Miss M. McLENING

Howitt Secondary School,

Loscoe Road,

Heanor, Derbyshire.

SCHOOL REPORT

Tel : Langley Mill 2055

Date   July 1960

Name   NARVEL ANNABLE.

Positions of Responsibility

1st.,2nd.,3rd. Swimming Certificates.

Behaviour   Attendance

Excellent   Excellent

Class Results

History   -   2nd.
Woodwork   -   4th.
Art   -   Very Good

Position in Class   Number in Class
7th.   26

General Remarks

Narvel is a boy who thinks for himself and is of above average
intelligence but his standard of
academic work is below this
standard. He has no aptitude for
Maths., but is capable of fluent
self-expression though his spelling
is poor. He is very reliable.

M. McLening

190

Heanor Annals

1086 - In the Domesday Survey, a mention of a place called 'Hainoure' which means - 'high ridge'.

1400 - At some point in this century, Heanor's most famous landmark is built. The tower of St Lawrence's Church is visible for many miles along the Erewash valley.

1700 - This century sees the building of the original Heanor Hall near the Market Place on the site of the present South East Derbyshire College. This was the home of the rich Fletcher family who owned local coal mines.

1801 - Population of Heanor is 1,061.

1848 - Opening of the new Church of England National School for working class children on High Street. Sometimes referred to as 'The Penny School'.

1849 - Birth of Alfred Edward Miller Mundy who was to become the Squire of Shipley Hall in 1877.

1850 - About the beginning of rapid industrial development in this hill town whose increasing population is now just under 4,000. Chief growing industries are - coal mines, hosiery and brick making.

1867 - Heanor Town Hall built.

1869 - The man who gave his name to Ray Street, John Ray of Heanor Hall dies. The estate is bought by Edward Miller Mundy of Shipley Hall.

1870 - Education Act of Gladstone's Liberal ministry. WE Forster said that the object was to complete the present voluntary system of existing elementary schools by filling up the gaps.

1880 - Compulsory attendance was introduced for all children from the age of five to ten.

1881 - Heanor population has reached 8,000.

1888 - The shops and buildings on the south side of Red Lion Square are erected, including the flat once occupied by the author 1957-58. Much of Heanor as we know it today was constructed in these few years.

1890 - The Market Place is laid out on park land from Heanor Hall estate, given by Mr Edward Miller-Mundy of Shipley Hall. The very first building, a restaurant and later the Ripley Co-op, was erected on the site of the present Police Station.
August Bank Holiday - Daniel Stirland, standing on the recreational ground (now the Town Ground); is suddenly struck dead by lightening! Verdict returned by the coroner - *"An Act of God!"*

1891 - **November 2nd** - Mundy Street Church of England Boys School opens with Mr Henry Dix appointed as the first headmaster who would serve 24 years up to 1915. There were 189 boys on the books.
Heanor population is now 9,779.

1894 - Heanor Hall becomes a Technical School with Mr Ralph Stoddard as the first Headmaster.

1895 - Bulmers Trade Directory describes Heanor as - ".... an extensive and prosperous parish which lies on the coal measures." The Northern and Midland Railway pass through the town.
August 20th. Birth of Miss Maud Earnshaw at Smalley.

1899 - The school leaving age was raised from ten to twelve.

1900 - Heanor's first telephone was installed at Nevilles Garage - Langley Mill 1!

1901 - **January** - The death of Queen Victoria, after a reign of 64 years, brings to an end the age to which she gave her name. Edward VII becomes the new king at the age of 59. The Heanor population rises to 12,418.

1902 - An Education Act created Local Education Authorities responsible for building and maintaining the free elementary and, for the first time, state maintained secondary schools. All secondary schools charged fees and therefore only the better off could afford to send their children to fee paying - private, grammar, or the more prestigious 'public' schools.

December - Birth of Doris Higton (later Mrs Doris Cook).

1904 - Most, but not all Heanor homes are now supplied with piped pure drinking water to replace local wells. Bath night was Friday in front of the fire in the zinc tub. The 'un-named' source states that piped water was available as early as 1860.

1905 - Public gas lighting is installed in Heanor.
Birth of Leonard Smith.

1907 - Free places were introduced for the cleverest children of the elementary schools, later came to be known as 'scholarships'. It was intended that a quarter of all places would be reserved for poor pupils who did well, but in practice it came to be less than one in twenty.
Mr Cootes describes the introduction of free places as -
   "The building of an educational ladder, which could be climbed
   by able and hard working children from any social background."

Marlpool Boys School, Claramount Road, Langley, opened for business. Mr Edward Hollingsworth, the first headmaster carried on for the next 38 years up to 1945.

1910 - Heanor Hall Technical School is demolished to make way for a new purpose built academy which was to become known as the Heanor Secondary School, and later the Heanor Grammar School.
Fred Buxton starts to show the very first moving pictures at his 'Picture Palace' in the Town Hall.

May - After a nine year reign, Edward VII dies. George V becomes the new King.

1911 - The Empire Theatre is built at Red Lion Square.

1912 - Power cables are installed for the trams. A few fortunate Heanorians have the new electric light, but most still use coal gas for illumination. It will be a further 44 years before Mundy Street Boys School has mains electricity! Philip Eggleshaw speaks of only three motor cars in the whole town. Mr Joe Mee is born.

1913 - The electric trams start to run.

1914 - **June** 25th - Visit of King George V and Queen Mary to Heanor. Huge celebrations with all school children being presented with a medal and a free tea!
August - the start of the First World War.

1915 - February 1st, the New Council School (Loscoe Road School) is opened with Henry Dix, from Mundy Street School, now the headmaster of the boys section. Mr Boam is appointed as the second headmaster of Mundy Street Boys School. The birth of Mary McLening.

1916 - Philip Eggleshaw recalls the Great War -
"Many local lads were killed in terrible conditions. One night several of us boys were solving the country's troubles under a lamp post on Ray Street, when we heard a loud noise and almost immediately the lamps went out. At first we thought the gas works had been destroyed, but then we realised it was a German Zeppelin air raid."
April 10th - First reference in the Loscoe Road School log to Miss Maud Earnshaw who will give the school 44 years of service.

1917 - **March** 1st - Winifred A Westland becomes, for the next 31 years, the headmistress of Loscoe Road Girls School.
May - Mr Boam the headmaster, and other teachers of Mundy Street Boys School are called up to fight in the 1914-18 Great War. Mr Lane will take over for the two years up to 1919.

1918 - The school leaving age was raised from twelve to fourteen. Former Mundy Street pupil Sergeant William Gregg was awarded the Victoria Cross. He was born in 1890 and worked as a miner at Shipley Colliery.

1919 - **February** - Mr Boam returns to his post and will remain until his death in 1943, making a total service of 26 years.

1920 - The death of Alfred Edward Miller Mundy, the last Lord of Shipley Hall and owner of most of Heanor.

1921 - First mention in the Mundy Street Boys School log book of W. Smith (Billy Smith) as an 'uncertified teacher'. He becomes an 'uncertified master' in 1922.

1922 - 'The Cosy', the first purpose built cinema is opened on the Market Place, and well remembered by a nine year old Joe Mee who was one of the first in to enjoy the silent films.
Mr Charles Mettam becomes the headmaster of Loscoe Road Boys School for the next 16 years.

1924 - Maud Earnshaw at the age of 29 gets married to Adam, and emerges as the formidable - Mrs Buxcey!

1926 - The Hadow Report criticised 'all age schools' where children spent their entire school lives in the same building. It proposed separate infant school from five to seven, and a junior school up to age 11. An examination (the future 11+) would determine what type of secondary school would suit them best. Birth of Eric Wardle.

1927 - First reference in the Loscoe Road School log to Hubert Charles Chambers and Maurice Brentnall.

1928 - **September** 28th - Miss Crumpton leaves her post at Loscoe Road Girls School to become the headmistress of the newly built wooden Lockton Avenue Girls School.

1929 - Birth of Peter Crofts.

1930 - Miss Minnie Large first mentioned in the Mundy Street Boys School log book. Heanor population now 22,482.

1931 - Electric trams were replaced by electric trolley buses. The journey from Ripley to Nottingham took one and a half hours.
September Eric Wardle aged 5 starts Loscoe Road Infants School.
October - Doris Higton marries Percy Ward Cook.

1934 - Eric Wardle moves up to Loscoe Road Boys School.

1936 - **January** - George V dies and Edward VIII is the new King.
September - Peter Crofts, aged seven, attends at Mundy Street Boys School.
December - Since his partner Mrs Simpson is not allowed to become Queen Wallis, Edward abdicates and his brother ascends the throne as King George VI. His wife Elizabeth, still alive today, is better known as the dear old Queen Mother.

1937 - **April** 5th - Mr Charles Mettam retires, and Jasper Augustus Strover is appointed as the new headmaster of Loscoe Road Boys School. The first Dandy Comic is on sale for tuppence. If you still own a copy, it is worth three thousand pounds!

1938 - **April** 4th - Mr LK Jeffery becomes a new master at Loscoe Road Boys School. The first Beano Comic is on sale.

1939 - September - World War II, Air Raid shelters dug in the Loscoe Road School gardens.

1940 - Eric Wardle leaves Loscoe Road School at the age of 14. Peter Crofts leaves Mundy Street Boys School and attends the Heanor Grammar School.

1941 - Barry Forster becomes a pupil at Mundy Street Boys School

1943 - **February** - Mr Boam the headmaster of Mundy Street Boys School died. Mr Leonard Smith is appointed as the third Headmaster who will have the longest tenure of 27 years up to 1970.
Shipley Hall is demolished.

1944 - The Butler Education Act implemented the above Hadow Report of 1926 and would provide free secondary education for all pupils.
Douglas Nicholls in the Artillery, is wounded in France.

1945 - April 30th - Hitler shoots himself and World War II is over.
One third of a pint of free school milk was provided for every child. Local Education Authorities had to provide school meals - but no slugs! July 12th Narvel Annable is born. July 16th the first atomic bomb is exploded and Barry and Derek Goostrey are born. July 18th Horace Hart is born.

1947 - The school leaving age was raised from fourteen to fifteen years. Mrs Doris Cook joins the staff of Loscoe Road Girls School. Peter Crofts, aged 18, leaves the Heanor Secondary School which is now known as the Heanor Grammar School. Little Pam Carter battles with the big snow fall; and when that's gone - a future Chancellor of the Exchequer takes a ride around Heanor on three wheels!

1948 - **January** - Miss Westland retires and Miss Mary McLening is appointed as the new headmistress of Loscoe Road Girls School. She and the school share the same age.
November 30th - New blocks of 'hut' classrooms are built at Loscoe Road Girls School and one of them will become for all time - Mrs Cook's class.
December - Barry Forster leaves Mundy Street Boys School.
Middlesex County Council announced three new schools which will take all pupils without an entrance exam modelled on the American high school. The schools at Hillingdon and Potters Bar were referred to a 'comprehensives'.

1949 - Pam Carter starts Heanor Grammar School.

1951 - The old School Certificate was abolished and replaced with the new General Certificate of Education (GCE). To obtain the School Certificate it had been necessary to take examinations in several subjects and achieve a sufficient average level to graduate or 'matriculate'. The new GCE allowed the student to demonstrate ability in separate subjects at ordinary or advanced levels. Hence people of my generation would proudly speak of how many 'O' or 'A' levels they had accrued. The GCE mainly lived in the grammar schools.
The Memorial Park is opened by the Duke of Devonshire.

1952 - **February** - George V dies and our present Queen Elizabeth ascends the throne.

1953 - The last trolley buses ran through Heanor.
June - On a cold and wet Tuesday, a colourful and splendid Coronation for Elizabeth II. This is probably the year when the large trees were cut down at Mundy Street Boys School.

1954 - The Annables leave Belper and move to Heanor just before Christmas. Mary Watson is the Head Girl at the Heanor Grammar School. Heanor population now 24,000. Miss Freda Brentnall is appointed to her post at the Loscoe Road Girls School.

1955 - The Burnham Committee which set teachers pay, recommends that, in stages, the salary of a schoolmistress should be raised to equal a schoolmaster. I remember Mr Maurice Brentnall commenting that in his opinion this measure had depressed the pay levels of the profession.
January - Narvel Annable aged 9 starts Mundy Street Boys School.
April - Churchill resigns and Sir Anthony Eden becomes the new Prime Minister.
July - Pam Carter leaves Heanor Grammar School.
September - Aldercar Secondary Modern opens with Miss Beryl Briggs as the Senior Mistress.

1956 - The headmaster of Eton School warned that the growing number of comprehensive schools were a threat to the quality of British education. This issue is dealt with in Chapter 7.
April - Electricity is installed in Mundy Street Boys School. Mr Peter Crofts leaves the staff - bad news for the author.
June - Author takes and fails his Eleven Plus Examination. Great excitement at the Heanor Empire Cinema when 'Rock Around the Clock' a popular film arrives staring Bill Haley. Teddy Boy riots in some cities. Elvis Presley criticised as "Singularly distasteful".
September - Mary Watson takes up her first post at Loscoe Road Girls School.
October - Suez Crisis.

1957 - **January** - Eden resigns due to the Suez Crisis. Our young Queen sends for Harold Macmillan to be the new Prime Minister, not Mr Butler. Staff shortage crisis at Mundy Street Boys School, the author's class had to double up creating a class of more than 70 boys.
April - The Annables move down hill a few doors to a larger flat, at 4 Red Lion Square.
July - At an economic high point, Mr Macmillan tells the nation - *"You've never had it so good!"* This was not yet apparent in Heanor, and in personal terms the author had never had it so bad!

198

September - The Asian Flu epidemic hits Mundy Street Boys School causing smaller classes. Mr Douglas Nicholls filled in for a short period.

October - Russia launched Sputnik I, the first artificial earth satellite.

December - The United States attempt to launch a satellite is a spectacular disaster for the Americans and the author!

1958 - January - Mr Douglas Nicholls is appointed as a full time teacher at Mundy Street Boys School.

July - Beginning of the 'Sea Change' when at the age of 13, Narvel Annable leaves Mundy Street Boys School and starts the new William Howitt Secondary Modern School in September. 'Annabel' is given up as a bad job and Connie Annable obtains a place selling ladies clothes at 'Jeanett', Friargate, Derby.

September 1st - the birth of William Howitt Secondary Modern School.

Miss Mary Watson (to become Mrs Holmes in 1959) brings a group of girls up from what was the old Loscoe Road Girls School to change Mundy Street into a mixed School.

December - The Annables move away from Heanor and return to Stanley Common the birthplace of the author.

1959 - The first sensuous spring followed by a long hot glorious summer.

September - The author receives an unwelcome promotion out of the cosy world of Mrs Doris Cook and into the 'A' class of Mr Maurice Brentnall.

1960 - April - The coming of Horace, the birth of 'Dobba' and four precious happy months.

July - Sad school leaving to the strains of Adam Faith singing - 'From Now Until Forever'. Mrs Maud Buxcey retires from William Howitt Secondary Modern School.

1963 - The author emigrates to the United States on the original 1936 Queen Elizabeth Liner, and arrives one day before the assassination of President John F. Kennedy.

1964 - The new Labour Government had a policy of amalgamating grammar and secondary modern schools in new units called the comprehensive school, which would end the 11+ exam and accept all pupils of all abilities. Closing down the Heanor Grammar School and William Howitt Secondary Modern in 1964 to open up Heanor Gate Comprehensive School - was the result. Death of Barry Goostrey.

1965 - The GCE examinations had been criticised for being too difficult for many pupils of average ability. A new easier Certificate of Secondary Education was introduced designed to cater for the Secondary Modern School. This qualification had elements of 'continual assessment' with project work to take the pressure of the 'be and end all' final examination of the GCE two year course. Consequently the CSE became a poor cousin to the more prestigious GCE, even though a top Grade I CSE was supposed to be equivalent to a GCE 'C' grade pass. From personal experience as a form tutor as well as a class teacher, I can say that on the whole, employers did not rate the top CSE as an 'O' Level.

1970 - Mr Leonard Smith retires from Mundy Street School after 27 years service as the headmaster, and is replaced by Mr Ian Ottewell the fourth headmaster.

1973 - The school leaving age was raised to 16 years.

1975 - July - Miss Mary McLening retires from William Howitt Junior Community School after 28 years of service.
September - Having graduated from Eastern Michigan University, the author took up his first appointment teaching history at a private Catholic academy - St Bridget High School in Detroit.

1977 - Miss Mary McLening is tragically killed in a car crash.

1978 - The author begins his seventeen year span in the history department of a large British comprehensive school. The first eight years were under a traditional headmaster, and in the final nine years a progressive headteacher made changes which are criticised in this book.

1979 - The death of Mr Leonard Smith at the age of 74.

1981 - July - Mr Douglas Nicholls retires from Mundy Street School after 23 years full time service.

1983 - The Heanor Empire Cinema is closed and demolished soon afterwards.

1984 - The GCE and the CSE were replaced by the new exam - the General Certificate of Secondary Education.

1994 - **December** - Mr Ian Ottewell retires from Mundy Street School after 24 years service.

1995 - **April** - Narvel Annable retires from his comprehensive school after 17 years of service.

1997 - **March** - The death of Mr Peter Crofts at the age of 67.

After 1960

William Howitt Secondary Modern School did not cease to exist when I left. It lived on another four years up to the July of 1964. Mr Tom J. Larimore started in September 1960 and taught history in Heanor for the following 34 years. He is a principal contributor to the Heanor and District Local History Society. Ian McIntyre, the art teacher and well known local artist started at the same time.

In this 1961 photograph below, Mr Larimore is the teacher seated. The only known pupil is Jenny Keys nee Beeston, on the back row 6th from the left.

Bibliography

BBC Timewatch	*Grammar School Boys - 14.4.98.*
Bulmers.	*Trade Directory 1895.*
Cootes, R.J.	*Britain since 1700.*
Crofts & Read.	*Footsteps through Smalley.*
Dickens, Charles.	*A Christmas Carol*
Derbyshire County Council.	*The Gardens of Shipley Hall.*
Derbyshire Record Office, Matlock.	*Mundy Street Boys School Log Book.*
Heanor and District Local History Society.	*Heanor Street Names (1977)*
	Two Centuries of Transport (1978)
	Around Old Heanor (1982)
	Life in Old Heanor (1983)
	Heanor Then and Now (1987)
	A History of Mining in the Heanor Area (1993)
Loscoe Road School	*Log Books*
Kindersley, Dorling.	*Chronicle of the 20th Century*
Mee, Arthur.	*Derbyshire.*
Page, W.	*A Victorian History of Derbyshire.*
Pedley, Robin.	*The Comprehensive School.*
Shakespeare.	*As You Like It.*
	Much Ado About Nothing.
	The Tempest.
Un-named.	*The History of Mundy Street Boys School in Heanor, Derbyshire, from 1891 to 1944.*

The extracts from BRITAIN SINCE 1700, by Richard Cootes are reprinted by permission of Addison Wesley Longman Ltd.

"From Now Until Forever" Words and Music by Max Nesbitt, Harry Nesbitt and Geoffrey Venis. 1958 Carlin Music Corporation, Iron Bridge House, 3 Bridge Approach, London NW8. Used by permission.

Acknowledgements

The author would like to thank the following for kindly
giving up time and providing valuable information.

Brian Annable, Molly Annable, Frank Bacon, Brian Brailsford, Beryl
Briggs, Barry Brough, Cynthia Brown, Jim Brown, Stanley Buxcey,
Pam Carter, Malcolm Caulton, Freda Cirillo, Joyce Clay, The Rt. Hon.
Kenneth Clarke, QC, MP. Barry Cook, Kathleen Cook, Joyce Crofts,
Peter Crofts, Jim Ferraby, Barry Forster, Kelvin Gibbs, Derek
Goostrey, Horace Hart, Janet Hart, Valerie Hodson, Michael Hogg,
Mary Holmes, Roger Hull, Philip Justice, Jenny Keys, Tom Larimore,
Derek Limer, John March, His Honour Judge Keith Matthewman, Q.C.
Joe Mee, Terry Miles, Douglas Nicholls, Roy Palmer, Dawn Payne,
Don Poundall, Jeffrey Ratcliffe, Sheila Rouse, Winifred Molly Smith,
Ronald Stanley, Freda Staley, Terry Sullivan, Kath Syson, Eric Wardle,
Graham Waterall, John Wright and Margaret Wright. Thanks also to
those who have helped but prefer not to be named.

Photographs and Documents

The following have generously loaned precious property.
Brian Brailsford, Stanley Buxcey, Barry Cook, Joyce Crofts, Barry
Forster, Derek Goostrey, Horace Hart, Jenny Keys, David Martin, Keith
Matthewman, Joe Mee, Terry Miles, Douglas Nicholls, Roy Palmer,
Dawn Payne, Ronald Stanley and Eric Wardle.

Proof-readers

Victor Bamford, Terry Durand, Keith and Jane Matthewman.

By the same author ...

"Miss Calder's Children"
A Social History of Belper, Biography and Critique on Modern Education
ISBN 0 9530419 0 5

This book is about the author's first teacher, the formidable and greatly respected mistress who taught for half a century at the long since demolished Bridge House School. Narvel Annable makes frequent critical contrast between present day and traditional classroom practices, based on his personal experiences of 17 years in a large comprehensive school at the sharp edge of the chalk face. This is supported by a foreword from Nick Seaton, the Chairman of the Campaign for Real Education.

The biography, involving 20 photographs dating from 1871, is compiled from mostly primary sources including some elderly Beaurepeirians who can still recall the Victorian Calder sisters of popular living memory.

Described by the Belper News (2.7.97) as -

"A superb insight as to how the education system developed within Belper, and how children learnt their values of life. There are unique snippets of various historical events and places recorded, now long gone. A time-capsule of experiences to be read and appreciated by many generations to come. An invaluable document to be added to the rich history of Belper, and also a 'must' for all those involved with the education of our children. I enjoyed this book."

Pauline Oldrini.